MW01031827

# THE PRESENCE OF ANGELS IN YOUR LIFE

# THE PRESENCE OF ANGELS IN YOUR LIFE

Cheryl and Harry Salem

DESTINY IMAGE® PUBLISHERS, INC.
P.O. Box 310, Shippensburg, PA 17257-0310
*"Speaking to the Purposes of God for This Generation and for the Generations to Come."*

This book and all other Destiny Image, Revival Press, Mercy Place, Fresh Bread, Destiny Image Fiction, and Treasure House books are available at Christian bookstores and distributors worldwide.

Previously published by Harrison House copyright 1997 as
*An Angel's Touch* Previous ISBN: 1-57794-328-7

For a U.S. bookstore nearest you, call 1-800-722-6774.
For more information on foreign distributors, call 717-532-3040.
Or reach us on the Internet: www.destinyimage.com

Trade Paper ISBN 13: 978-0-7684-3637-2
Hardcover ISBN 13: 978-0-7684-3638-9
Large Print ISBN 13: 978-0-7684-3639-6
Ebook ISBN 13: 978-0-7684-9041-1

For Worldwide Distribution, Printed in the U.S.A.
1 2 3 4 5 6 7 8 9 10 11 / 15 14 13 12 11

# DEDICATION

This book is dedicated to our three earthly "angels": Harry III, Roman, and Gabrielle, who now lives in Heaven. Thank you for always believing in and being patient with Mom and Dad. We love you!

# CONTENTS

# INTRODUCTION

What would you think if an apparently completely normal and well-adjusted person walking down the street stopped you and said, "I had one leg that was almost two inches shorter than the other, and God instantaneously made my short leg grow out to match the other"? Or maybe this person said to you, "When I was a little girl, the milkman said I was going to be Miss America." Or how about this one: "I see angels by the hundreds, even thousands, and I even see them in brilliant color." There was a time when I would have said, "If you don't turn and walk away—no, run away—you must be as crazy as they are."

Well, if that person was my wife, Cheryl, I would tell you to think twice before you walk away. You see, Cheryl was told by her family's milkman that she would be Miss America someday. And this was before she was in a terrible car accident that left her with over 150 stitches in her face and a leg crushed so badly the doctors said she might never walk again. And, yes, God did divinely heal her scars, gave her a new bone in her leg, and six years later miraculously lengthened her short leg two inches. In 1980 Cheryl *was* crowned Miss America and has shared her testimony of God's power and love with audiences around the world.

Even more amazing is the fact that God has opened Cheryl's eyes to see into the supernatural realm. She has seen lots and lots of angels, many, many times *and* in brilliant color. As I said, there was a time when I would have agreed that this is too strange. I'm a real facts-and-figures kind of man, and I see things in black and white. I have never seen an angel and I may never see one. But before you begin reading this book, I want you to know a little more about my wife. Cheryl is not a nut or someone who lights candles and sits around waiting for spooky, supernatural phenomena to occur. She is first a loving, supporting wife with a normal husband. She is the mother of three normal, well-adjusted children. Harry and Roman are with us here, but our daughter, Gabrielle, went to be with Jesus in November of 1999. Cheryl took them to Little League, to the YMCA for basketball, picked them up from school, helped them with their homework, and disciplined them when they needed it. She is as normal as anyone in your own family, maybe even more so.

Cheryl is rooted—rooted in the Word of God. For that very reason, her story is factual and real. She isn't like Hollywood's version of people who dabble in the supernatural, usually the "dark side" that scares the "hell" into people. (Instead of delivering them from it, it drives them to it!) The world has seen too much of that side of the supernatural, and our young people are being lured into so much deception they think it is "cool" and a turn-on. Neither is she going to tell you about cute little baby angels (cherubs) to be put on a shelf and worshiped.

Cheryl's experiences in seeing angels are as real as it gets. She started seeing angels before all the hoopla and the increasing number of books were written about angels, before it was on *Time* magazine's cover, before the "angel craze" hit the gift shops. But when she first began to share with me what she was seeing, there was never a moment of doubt in my mind that what she was seeing was from God and was real.

Cheryl has been walking in faith her entire life—walking and expecting God to reveal Himself to her through healings and unexplainable miracles in her life and in the lives of others. Add to that fact, she was a crippled, scarred, poor little girl in a wheelchair, living on a dirt road in Mississippi who became Miss America, a title held by less than 90 women in the world. A title so coveted by little girls and young women that many of them would do anything to get it and do anything, after the fact, to keep it. And through it all, Cheryl has remained humble and solidly grounded in God's Word to fulfill His purpose for her life. I believe this is why God has allowed her to see past and through the natural into the supernatural realm and has revealed the angels to her.

Don't think for one minute that you can't see angels. The angels are there even if you can't see them. They are as close as your breath on a mirror. They are there for you and for me, as Cheryl will tell you in this book. They are not to be worshiped, and you can't tell them what to do. I believe Cheryl's telling of her experiences and the scriptural studies she has added will enlighten you and answer many questions you have about angels.

You see, God has a plan for everything, and the experiences shared in this book are part of God's plan for Cheryl's and my life. Believe me when I say it would have been a lot easier if these "angel" experiences hadn't happened in our lives. But they did.

And, yes, I have questioned why she sees the angels in our home and I don't. To be honest with you, I know now that I was not in the position spiritually to see them or to understand why I was seeing them when this all began. But I believe I will see them someday and be able to grasp the *why*—not question the *when*. And I believe the same for you.

*— Harry Salem II*

# I

## AND MY EYES WERE OPENED...

Get ready! You are going to "see" the angels through Cheryl's eyes. When I read her description of the angels in this chapter, all I could say was yes! You will, too!

— *Harry Salem II*

It was a day like any other day in Buffalo, New York, in early June of 1992. The breeze in the air was warm, and the city was echoing the sounds of the summer—kids playing in the parks, people eating at outdoor restaurants, and the tourists on vacation. The sun was shining, and we were well prepared for the crusade that was ahead of us in the evening service. Everything had been set up in advance, and Harry had meticulously made sure every detail was ready. No stone that could potentially cover a problem had been left unturned. Yes, we could relax because tonight was going to be fantastic.

The service began as I shared my testimony with an anticipatory crowd and sang a few songs to help usher in the presence of God. The singers led the people into a glorious time of praise and worship. As the swell of music and singing engulfed the atmosphere, it became obvious this was going to be a uniquely wonderful service in the presence of God. I was on the platform, basking in the unity that prevailed throughout the auditorium. The place was saturated with the love of God.

The people were already responding to God's sweet flow of anointing. They were raising their hands and singing, with the literal glow of the Holy Spirit on their upturned faces. God was here, and He was in charge of this service.

It was as if God had poured Himself out onto the people—He had anointed the whole room with His very presence. Tonight was going to be special, and there was no demon in hell that could stop it!

All of a sudden, I felt an overwhelming presence of the peace of God. I felt the entrance of His power—that sweet, almost breathtaking feeling that comes when you know you are no longer in charge. God Almighty had come on the scene. I felt that rush of excitement in my spirit as I looked up and saw the most beautiful entrance of two thousand or more angelic beings into the sanctuary! With bursts of light, they came through the walls and ceiling as if nothing was there to prevent their entrance. The upper half of the auditorium was completely crowded with angels! There were so many splendid angelic creatures that they looked like a sea of angels.

They were warriors. Every one of them had something in their hands. Some had hand-to-hand combat weapons. They appeared to hold things like knives, swords, shields, and many other objects obviously used in battle, but I was unable to identify the weapons. I noticed that a few of the angels had no weapons but were holding in their hands musical instruments that looked like trumpets. They looked as if they were waiting for their signal to play.

I stared at the ceiling in complete wonder and amazement. Although God had allowed me to see angels a few times in the past, this was the first time my eyes had beheld the splendor of God's angels in such color and magnitude. It was so real to my eyes that I just knew everyone in the building could see exactly what I was seeing. It didn't occur to me I might be the only one who was seeing this spectacular phenomena in the spirit realm.

The angels were standing shoulder to shoulder, flanked like soldiers at attention facing in toward the center of the sanctuary. All of a sudden, a group of about 50 would turn their backs to us and begin to fight an unseen adversary. The enemy from outside seemed to be trying to enter the building, and it appeared to be the job of the angels to defend the premises and keep the demonic force out. This angelic force of about 50 or so swished out of the ceiling, leaving the remains of colored light particles dissipating in the air. It was as if they had gained the advantage in the warfare, and in "hot pursuit" they pushed the demonic forces beyond the walls of the building!

I could hear the activity of the angelic realm, and it was a war going on right in the middle of the preaching! The clinking of metal against metal as weapons struck one another reverberated throughout the recesses of my spirit's ears. There were definitely the sounds of war in this place. They were not talking. They were not singing. They were not shouting. They were fighting. And yet

I had no fear. None at all! Somehow I knew the angels were well capable of handling this situation.

There was more than one battle going on here. The obvious battle (to me) of angelic beings of light and demonic beings of darkness was heating up the very spiritual atmosphere. But there was also a battle going on right inside my head! I was seeing and hearing the natural realm and seeing and hearing the supernatural realm all at the same time. I wanted to shout, "Wait! What's happening here?" And yet I knew this was no time for questions and no time for doubt.

I pushed through my natural thinking and forced myself not to analyze what I was seeing. I chose to watch by faith so I would not lose sight of what God was doing. I was being allowed the privilege of being a spectator to the miraculous, wonder-working power of God through His angels, and I didn't want to miss a thing!

While the group of angels that was now outside the building was in combat, the remaining thousands of angels were standing around the entire perimeter of the auditorium in a position that resembled a military stance of protection. It reminded me of the scenes I have seen when the president of the United States was about to enter a room and the Secret Service preceded him and "stood guard," constantly surveying the situation for security purposes.

I still was not afraid. In fact, I never had any fear at all. The atmosphere was filled with peace and tranquility, and the exhilaration of the anointing and presence of God absolutely permeated my entire being. There just wasn't any room in my emotions for fear!

In a few moments I saw the same regiment of angels that had exited through the ceiling in pursuit of the unseen enemy outside the building settle back through the ceiling and fall into formation with the other angelic beings. Shoulder to shoulder they stood, watching every move in the natural realm and the supernatural realm. Nothing seemed to go unnoticed by their trained eyes and ears.

I could see them as plainly as I could see the pastor, but it was an unusual "seeing." I could look right at them, and yet I could see right through them, too! I could make out their forms, details about them, their overall appearances, and yet I was looking into light that was reflecting off them.

Their features were remarkable! They were between 9 and 12 feet tall, varying in heights and sizes. This was quite easy to assess since, at that time, my husband was standing in the back of the service, watching to make sure everything was running smoothly. Harry was leaning against the back wall of the auditorium when the angels entered the building. It was so simple to compare the height of the angels to my husband's 6-foot 1-inch frame as he was directly under them.

Some were almost double Harry's height. Some were a little less than double his height, and some seemed to be a little more than double. They were very muscular, beautifully proportioned, and well defined in their forms. They all appeared as male, even though now, after several years of study, I have found that angels are genderless.[1]

*For in the resurrected state neither do [men] marry nor are [women] given in marriage, but they are like the angels in heaven* (Matthew 22:30).

They all had on different-colored apparel, quite nondescript, but it seemed to be comfortable, loose fitting, and not confining. Some of the shirts were like pullovers and others were loose-fitting vests. Some of the pants were below the knee and others went all the way to their feet. Some had on shoes and others did not. Their forms were not always completely distinguishable. The shoes were simple, like sandals or house slippers. All of their appearances were similar, but no two looked exactly alike.

All of the angels had some type of waistband around their midsection. Some of the "belts" were bright and shiny like gold and others were indistinguishable. Some of the waist pieces seemed to hold a type of sheath for their weapons.

As I have pondered their appearances over the last few years, it has come to me that it would be like trying to describe the human race by describing one person. That is almost impossible. Even though we have many similarities, we are all very different to the eye, and so are the angels. God truly is a God of variety and tastes!

The colors the angels exuded were magnificent! They ranged from brilliant purples, reds, fuchsias, and greens, to almost every color of the rainbow. This was such a surprise to me. What little I knew about angels up to this point in my life, I thought they were all like a very brilliant white light. Yet, in reality, to look at them was like looking into a spotlight but with a colored gel over the light. They were definitely reflecting God's glory from being in His presence.

Each angelic being was radiating light in every color you can imagine. Even though they were radiating light, I could still distinguish their facial and bodily features. Every one of them was extremely handsome and beautifully sculpted in figure and form. They had very defined, almost rugged, facial features, with different hair lengths and styles. They were all distinct and unique in appearance. There was something about them that was shining from the very depths of their beings that overpowered their appearance.

The greatest thing about their presence was not their appearance but the anointing of God they brought with them. The angels' presence brought peace, contentment, and absolute absence of fear. They were not smiling or frowning. They looked serious, as if they had a job or assignment to do, and they were concentrating on accomplishing it. There is no doubt in my mind they are very confident, yet vigilant. It is evident in their faces, in the way they stand; everything about them exudes confidence. I think that is why I never felt afraid. I just knew these servants sent from God were completely capable of handling any circumstance!

I have tried to think of "human" words to describe them, and it has been difficult. Seeing into the supernatural realm is kind of like looking into a film negative. You can see everything, and yet you can see what's behind it also. I have finally resigned myself to the fact that trying to describe the supernatural dimension with natural words and descriptions is almost impossible to accomplish. Although I know I can give you an idea of what I was seeing, it's still not even close to the magnitude of the spiritual realm of which I was privileged to partake with my eyes and ears.

The light that illuminates from them is impossible to describe accurately. It is brilliant and yet not overpowering. It is bright and yet warm. It is like trying to explain to someone before they experience salvation what it feels like to know that you are born again.

You just have to experience it to understand fully the dimension of it!

The illumination from the angels made me feel safe, warm, and protected. Now I realize the reason for this is because they come from the Father God, and His presence is reflecting through them, which explains the presence of light in their beings.

I was in awe of them, but I did not feel any desire to worship them. The Lord began to impress upon me by the Holy Spirit that I should not seek after them.

> But seek (aim at and strive after) first of all His kingdom and His righteousness (His way of doing and being right), and then all these things taken together will be given you besides (Matthew 6:33).

There was nothing I could do to make them come to me. I couldn't be spiritual enough or not spiritual enough. I couldn't deserve their appearance or not deserve their appearance. I believe God was trying to teach me that the angels are not to be worshiped, and they are not to be sought after. They are sent when the Father God chooses to send them. And we see them when the Father chooses for us to see them. We have absolutely nothing to do with it.

> Let no one defraud you by acting as an umpire and declaring you unworthy and disqualifying you for the prize, insisting on self-abasement and worship of angels, taking his stand on visions [he claims] he has seen, vainly puffed up by his sensuous notions and inflated by his unspiritual thoughts and fleshly conceit (Colossians 2:18).

*And I, John, am he who heard and witnessed these things. And when I heard and saw them, I fell prostrate before the feet of the messenger (angel) who showed them to me, to worship him. But he said to me, Refrain! [You must not do that!] I am [only] a fellow servant along with yourself and with your brethren the prophets and with those who are mindful of and practice [the truths contained in] the messages of this book. Worship God!* (Revelation 22:8-9).

This certainly took a big load of responsibility off my shoulders and made me realize that I was not special, either. This was what the Father God had chosen to do, and my only choice in the whole matter was whether I was going to be obedient or not in telling the people what *God* wanted me to tell them and to give God the worship—not the angels.

The Bible plainly tells us that anything that comes out of the angel's mouth is sent from the Father and is not a message from the angel itself but from the Father God. The angel is just a messenger.

*Bless (affectionately, gratefully praise) the Lord, you His angels, you mighty ones who do His commandments, harkening to the voice of His word. Bless (affectionately, gratefully praise) the Lord, all you His hosts, you His ministers who do His pleasure* (Psalm 103:20-21).

When you receive a letter from a friend in the mail and she tells you that she loves you, you don't grab your mail carrier, give him a big hug and kiss and tell him you love him too, do you? The mail carrier didn't write and say he loves you. He just delivered the message.

And yet some people try to place deity on the angels, as if the angels are doing something or saying something of their own free will. The angels are only following the commands of their Master, the Father God. And we are the recipients.

So don't worship or be afraid of the messenger (the angel). Just enjoy the benefits that God has given us through these heavenly beings and learn all God has told us in His Word about them. Then you won't be surprised by anything that God does or be misled by any counterfeit satan may send to try and confuse you.

One of the most frequently asked questions about what I have seen is, "Do the angels have wings?" Some had wings and others did not. However, the wings did not seem to be their mode of transportation. They could "fly," as we would call it, because they could move about without the confines of walls, floors, and ceilings. I began to see and understand as I watched them that they are not dimensional like we are—they appeared to have no substance matter like we do. Because we are made up of earthly matter (substance), we cannot go through walls, etc.—therefore, we are dimensional. They are not confined to our space but truly are able to travel in any capacity necessary to perform their duties.

I can't say that the angels' wings were not used for flying, but it didn't seem necessary for them to have wings to move about. They did not stand with their wings spread, nor did they "flap" their wings when they fought or pursued the demonic enemy in combat. It was as if their wings tucked "in" somewhere when they weren't using them.

To say that I was stunned by all that I was seeing is putting it mildly. It's not like I see into the supernatural realm every day of my life. I was sitting on the platform with my mouth dropped open completely and, I am sure, with the most dumbfounded look on my face!

When I came to myself and realized what was happening, I grabbed my friend on the platform by the hand and said, "Can you see them? They are here by the thousands!" Of course, she had no idea what I was talking about. But by the look on my face, she knew I was excited and had something to share with her. I began describing what I was seeing, and she asked me if I knew why they were here. I said I didn't know, but I began to question the Lord immediately.

Please notice here that I didn't try to talk to the angels. They were ministering servants sent for us, the saints, and I somehow instinctively knew not to try to talk to them.

> *Are not the angels all ministering spirits (servants) sent out in the service [of God for the assistance] of those who are to inherit salvation?* (Hebrews 1:14)

They were busy doing their jobs, and I needed information, so I began to question the One who is my constant companion and friend—the precious Holy Spirit.

The Holy Spirit spoke to me and said the angels were sent to this meeting to protect the miracles. "To protect the miracles?" I questioned. The Holy Spirit impressed upon my heart that the angels were protecting the miracles from the onslaught of demonic attack that would keep God's people from receiving. I thought about this revelation, and then I remembered that a hard-rock music group, known for its blatant denial of God, was in concert just a few miles down the road. There were 60,000 in attendance. The traffic tie-ups alone were causing a battle for people trying to get to the church service. Perhaps there was more warfare in the heavenlies and protection needed than we realized.

I asked the Lord why this meeting was different from any other. The Holy Spirit gently, and yet ever so clearly, began to show me that angels are always where God's people are, and this meeting was no different except for the fact that I could see the angels. The Holy Spirit reminded me of the Scripture where the prophet Elisha and his servant were rescued through the help of many angels.

> *When the servant of the man of God rose early and went out, behold, an army with horses and chariots was around the city. Elisha's servant said to him, Alas, my master! What shall we do? [Elisha] answered, Fear not; for those with us are more than those with them. Then Elisha prayed, Lord, I pray You, open his eyes that he may see. And the Lord opened the young man's eyes, and he saw, and behold, the mountain was full of horses and chariots of fire round about Elisha* (2 Kings 6:15-17).

The mountain was full of angels on horses and chariots that had been there all the time—ready to help Elisha win this war. When Elisha prayed, God opened the eyes of the servant to see the invisible dimension to believe the impossible.

So you see, the angels are with us "at all times," not just when we can see them. God did a wonderful thing in Buffalo through the presence of the angels, but He would have done the same work whether I could have seen the angels or not!

## ENDNOTE

1. *Strong's Exhaustive Concordance of the Bible,* Angels, 14.

# 2

## PAINFUL OBEDIENCE!

Believe me, Cheryl and I have agonized over
this manuscript. She takes very seriously the
responsibility God has placed in her hands to
share the truth of what He has shown her in the
supernatural realm. She has been obedient to wait
upon His timing, and she gives God all the glory!
When you read this chapter, you will understand
what a woman of faith Cheryl has always been.

— *Harry Salem II*

I don't think anything has ever been harder for me than to put
this story on paper. Seeing the angels has been glorious, but telling *you* all I've seen through this book is obedience! My life will
never be the same. My eyes had been opened to another dimension—the supernatural realm of God. Whether I ever see into
that realm again or not, I know it exists, and God put it there for
us, His saints!

As I look back on my life, I seem to have always had the protection and direction of God's angels. There have been battles that would seem like defeat, such as the tragic car accident, devastating sexual abuse in my childhood, a miscarriage, the painful loss of our precious six-year-old daughter, Gabrielle Christian, and my battle with colon cancer. Some of the battles left scars to be healed and painful memories behind. But though there have been wounds and losses in the battle, I know through Christ this war has been won! And I see the majestic orchestration of the Master as He intermingled the natural life of a little naive country girl (with all the triumphs and tragedies) and the ever-active regions of the supernatural realm.

Even with the angelic assistance that I now know to have existed, I cannot say that my life has been easy or without tremendous effort to overcome the mountains set before me. My peaks and valleys may be of different heights, or degrees, or depths than yours, but they are nonetheless the despairs, anxieties, devastation, and exhilaration that have formed and shaped my life into what it is today. It is through these pressures that character has been and is being built in my life.

David says in Psalm 4:1, *"...You have freed me when I was hemmed in and enlarged me when I was in distress...."* I look back on my life now and I see problems, trials, and troubles squeezing the very life out of "Cheryl" so that less and less of me lives today and hopefully more and more of Jesus shines forth through me. I can see that through this squeezing I (like David) have been enlarged.

My entire life seems to have involved scaling one steep mountain after another. I was faced with impossible odds at 11 years old when I went through the windshield of a car in a tragic wreck. I had over 100 stitches in my face, my left leg was crushed, and my back was cracked. I was given very little hope of full recovery or of ever walking again.

I went through months of agony and almost unbearable pain while my body mended from its wounds. I cried out to the Lord in anguish for His help. He answered by performing a miracle—He put a bone in my left leg where there was no bone left. But because of the growth process of an 11-year-old girl, my left leg was almost 2 inches shorter than my right by the time the bone was formed and the miracle was completed. So from age 11 to age 17, others perceived me as a cripple—while I saw myself as a miracle! But God wasn't finished yet.

I asked Jesus to personally come into my heart and life at age 14. Yes, God healed my leg by putting a bone where there was none *before* I even knew Him as my personal Lord and Savior. What a loving Lord we serve! Oh, I had truly loved Jesus for years but had never actually made the personal commitment of my life to Him.

Then at 17 years old, I searched for God's answers to my physical problems and found God faithful again. He miraculously lengthened my left leg to be the same length as my right leg! I became a walking (and talking!) testimony of God's saving and healing power. I boldly declared what Jesus had done for me to anyone and everyone who would listen!

Then, to top off my already bizarre life, when I was a senior in high school, I felt the leading of God to enter beauty pageants. Imagine that announcement to family and friends: "God is calling me to pageants!" (That wasn't my earthly daddy's idea of being "called of God" to something!) Most of my friends and family thought I was crazy—especially when for five years I lost the pageants I entered! But because the Lord had ordered my steps, I finally walked the runway as Miss America 1980 for God's glory! These verses from Proverbs encouraged me: *"A man's heart plans his way, but the Lord directs his steps"* (Prov. 16:9 NKJV), and *"A man's steps are of the Lord; how then can a man understand his own way?"* (Prov. 20:24 NKJV).

No matter how many valleys we go through, I'm convinced there are still others to tread. I was Miss America, and I'm grateful to God for that experience. But today I'm so much more—wife, mother, preacher, speaker, singer, writer—and in all these things I'm a child of the King. There is life after Miss America, but the life that followed was faced with a totally different attitude than before.

As I have matured (women never say "grown older") and I look back on the valleys I have crossed, I see a wonderful thread running through the streams in the valleys. That thread is faith. It took faith to believe when no one else believed with me. It took faith to stare death and destruction in the face and say, "You will not have me." It took faith to continue climbing one mountain after another until the tops had been reached over and over again.

These are the roads of life. Up and down the mountains we will climb, crossing the valleys, and sometimes the deserts, without a glimpse of hope in sight. Do we stop and turn around? What for? There is nothing behind. Only ahead will we find the triumph we are all so desperately seeking—the crown of life! Yes. That's it. Not a crown made by the hands of man, but the crown we will wear for all eternity!

In order to stay in God's destiny and will for my life, I have stayed in His Word and listened to the voice of the Holy Spirit who dwells within me. I have dedicated my entire life to further the gospel of Jesus Christ through the blood of the Lamb and the word of my testimony. By God's grace I have not wavered in my walk with the Lord, and I have remained loyal and true to the call of Jesus Christ. This is not to say that I have not made some wrong choices along the way and paid the price for those decisions. But even in the middle of my seeming "failures," I stayed faithful to my Lord, and much more importantly than that...He remained faithful to me.

Throughout my lifetime I have always felt a deep, intimate relationship with the Lord and have pursued this with great desire. I know that Jesus is my Savior, my Lord, my King, my best friend, my confidant, my everything. I have put my hope, my faith, my love, and my trust completely in Him. This has not been without a great price, and I have made the choice to pay that price. As I'll explain throughout these pages, my faith levels and trust levels have been sorely tried! Yet my merciful and compassionate God has always worked things together for my good.

I have always wanted to be an asset to God's Kingdom and never a stumbling block to any person's walk with the Lord or his or her pursuit of godliness. Teaching about the spiritual realm based completely on the Word of God is not a problem. However, sharing some of the intimate details of these past few years about angels and seeing into the spiritual realms (the demonic and angelic wars that I have witnessed) is frankly just too personal for *my* comfort.

Yet God would not let up on me. He has impressed upon my heart to share these experiences with the Body of Christ to teach and to edify. I have asked God more than once over the last few years, "Why am I seeing and talking with the angels?" He has answered me, not in an audible voice, but in my spirit. He said the visitations weren't for me personally. He said He can trust me to share each visit from the angels with everyone with whom I come into contact. He said that He knows me so well and knows that I will be careful to provide the important details without embellishing the truth. So what I am about to share, I know God wants me to share—however uncomfortable I am with doing so.

I am so proud of the Father God, and I love to sing His praises wherever I go. No matter how small the miracle may seem to someone else, I am always quick to make sure no person takes the credit for what God has done and deserves to be praised for. Not for one minute would I give any angel the worship that only my Savior and Lord deserves! Since God has shown me these things, they must by definition not go against Scripture. The Word of God is always my final source of truth, and I have provided numerous scriptural references for your own study.

So here I am, baring my soul and making myself vulnerable to the onslaught of the media and the religious society. Nothing that I am about to write is in any way written with the intent to be controversial or to gain attention. What I believe God wants to accomplish through this book is enlightenment of the minds, hearts, and spirits of His people. I believe He wants us to know and recognize many great benefits made available to us as His children that we have not fully utilized as a Body of believers.

In these last days the onslaught of the enemy is getting more and more intense. We need access to every weapon available to us as believers. And unfortunately, so many people, even Christians, have not grasped the reality of the supernatural realm. God said in Psalm 91:11-12:

*For He shall give His angels charge over you, to keep you in all your ways. In their hands they shall bear you up, lest you dash your foot against a stone* (NKJV).

Yet for lack of knowledge and revelation of truth, we, as Christians, aren't walking in the full activation of God's benefits in our lives. The angels are a formidable weapon, ministering spirits sent from the Father God to help us accomplish our godly mission upon this earth and to help us fulfill the call of God upon each and every one of our lives!

So, just as Paul beseeched the Corinthians in Second Corinthians 10:3 to remember: *"For though we walk (live) in the flesh, we are not carrying on our warfare according to the flesh and using mere human weapons,"* I beckon you to allow the Holy Spirit to bring you awareness, enlightenment, and a deeper understanding that though we walk in a natural realm, we have access to the supernatural realm through the power of the Holy Spirit. My prayer is that God will open your eyes to the beauty of His glorious presence and realm.

# 3

# BACK TO BUFFALO

As soon as Cheryl started seeing the angels, she went to the Word and began searching for God's truth about angels. So get ready to "see" what Cheryl has seen and to read what the Word has to say about the angels. Cheryl is a great teacher of His Word!

— *Harry Salem II*

Looking back, you can see that God had prepared me through the trials and triumphs of my life for the revealing of the angels that began in Buffalo. What a tremendous service we had that night!

To finish the story, after I "picked my jaw up off the ground," I shared what I was seeing. (By the way, I was still seeing the entire ceiling of the building covered in angels, and they were definitely doing their job!) I went to the podium and told the people what I was seeing and what the Holy Spirit had revealed to me about the angels' presence in the service.

The power of the Lord to heal and deliver was incredible. The entire team, including camera crew and sound engineers, came out and began to lay hands on people and pray for them. There were so many people being blessed by the Lord that they were too numerous to count!

As we left the building hours after the service ended, the angels were still visible to me. Maybe they are always there, and I was just privileged to see them that night.

This was the beginning of a great summer of wonderful, anointed services that God had ordained. Satan will always try to stop God's people from accomplishing their tasks on earth, but God is always faithful to send ministering servants (angels) to help us.

*Are not the angels all ministering spirits (servants) sent out in the service [of God for the assistance] of those who are to inherit salvation?* (Hebrews 1:14)

The following passage in Daniel is one of the clearest Old Testament examples that demonic armies oppose God's purposes and that earthly struggles often reflect what is happening in the heavenlies:

*And [the angel] said to me, O Daniel, you greatly beloved man, understand the words that I speak to you and stand upright, for to you I am now sent. And while he was saying this word to me, I stood up trembling. Then he said to me, Fear not, Daniel, for from the first day that you set your mind and heart to understand and to humble yourself before your God, your words were heard,*

*and I have come as a consequence of [and in response to] your
words. But the prince of the kingdom of Persia withstood me for
twenty-one days. Then Michael, one of the chief [of the celestial]
princes, came to help me, for I remained there with the kings of
Persia* (Daniel 10:11-13).

Also, in Daniel 10:3 we see that prayer and fasting may have
affected the outcome: *"I ate no pleasant or desirable food, nor did any
meat or wine come into my mouth; and I did not anoint myself at all for
the full three weeks."*

Here is yet another example of an angel responding to prayer:

*And he, gazing intently at him, became frightened and said, What
is it, Lord? And the angel said to him, Your prayers and your
[generous] gifts to the poor have come up [as a sacrifice] to God
and have been remembered by Him* (Acts 10:4).

These Scriptures seem to indicate that our desire to understand and our humility and consistent prayers are important in
God releasing His angels to defeat the demonic forces. You may
be thinking, *I know those Scriptures, and I don't interpret them the same
way as you do.* This is my interpretation, and I stress *my* interpretation. You may not see it the same way. It's not important
what or who we do or don't see. What's important is that we
learn to appreciate every gift of the spirit realm that God has
created for our benefit. We must learn through His Word how to
tap into those resources and utilize them in the fight against our
enemies—satan and his demons.

I don't think it is merely a coincidence that the angel, in bringing the message to Cornelius, made reference to his prayers and his
generous gifts. I believe God had the angel say *your prayers and your
generous gifts,* so that Cornelius, and ultimately we, God's believers,

would understand better the correlation between prayers, giving, and angelic intervention. By praying and giving, Cornelius was submitting himself completely to God. His humility and desire to know and understand God better was shown through his actions. I believe God is much more interested in our motives than in our actions, but many times our actions exemplify our motives.

The Buffalo experience was the beginning of many visitations or appearances from the angels. The more I saw them the hungrier I became to learn more about them. I began to study God's Word to explain how, why, and what I was seeing! It's very important to back up with God's Word everything we see, feel, and do; but it is most important that we never become more consumed with the "things" of God than we do with our "relationship" with God.

No matter what God does or doesn't do in or through my life (whether I see the angels or I don't), I have learned never to put any-thing ahead of my private time and intimate relationship with my Father God. You can't base your relationship with the Father God on any religion, any church, any preacher or teacher, any person or thing—and certainly not on whether you see the angels or not. Your personal relationship with Him is what is really important in the long run. When you spend time in His presence and in His Word, then you will know the way in which you should go.

*And your ears will hear a word behind you, saying, This is the way; walk in it, when you turn to the right hand and when you turn to the left* (Isaiah 30:21).

# 4

# Do We Sometimes Lose a Battle?

Cheryl and I had never suffered a loss anything like this before. As we left the doctor's office, it began to sink into our minds and hearts—we lost our baby! At that moment, change started to come in both of us. Here you may ask, "Where were the angels in the midst of tragedy?" We have learned it is not for us to question why or when, but just to be thankful when they do what God sends them to do. God is faithful, and He saw us through!

— *Harry Salem II*

The summer of 1992 was glorious in the church services, but it was devastating in so many other ways. Since early June when I had seen the angels at the crusade in Buffalo, it seemed as though all literal hell had broken loose in my husband's and my life. Harry and I felt led to have another child, and we had conceived in the middle of June. Since carrying our sons, Harry and Roman, had been relatively simple pregnancies, we didn't expect anything different this time. We were not prepared for the coming attack. We weren't expecting anything like it! The demonic realm has made it quite obvious that it hates our very existence, and to think that it would not hate our seed would be utterly ridiculous. However, we still weren't looking for this onslaught of the enemy.

We were so intrigued by the appearance of the angels in the beginning of the summer that both of us had begun to study about angels in God's Word. Through the Scriptures we researched every avenue possible to understand what I had seen. To question and to prove what you see and hear in the spirit realm is the only way not to be deceived by the devil and his demons. Don't ever forget that God's Word warns us in Second Corinthians 11:14, *"...For Satan himself masquerades as an angel of light."* You see, every angel is not necessarily from God.

As the summer progressed, I saw the angels again in every service. They were similar in appearance and performance as they had been in Buffalo.

Even in our home, the angels were manifested to my "sight" many times at night just walking down the hallway toward our sons' room, or roaming the kitchen when only Li'l Harry and I would be up in the morning. I guess you could say they were just "hanging around"! I am only kidding! I doubt if the angels ever just hang around. The Bible is fairly specific about their duties, and just "hangin' out" doesn't seem to be one of them!

In July, I had been in Hawaii preaching in the International Women's Conference in Honolulu, and the move of God had been tremendous. I am always so amazed by the power of God and His marvelous manifestation of love toward His children.

As usual, there was no time to waste. I flew over, preached, and took a red-eye flight back home to be with Harry and the children. I have never worried about my flesh, and pushing it to the limit has always been the norm for me. Being pulled emotionally between the *call* of God on my life and the *call* to be a godly wife and mother had become a game of "tug of war" in my mind.

I was constantly questioning the Lord and asking Him where I was needed most. What was the best way to balance these two lives and get the maximum benefit out of both of them without hurting anyone involved? Are there easy answers for these types of questions? I certainly was not finding them. So I pushed too hard, slept very little, and drained my physical body of its very life force.

On the flight home from Hawaii, I began to hurt in the area of my female organs, and I was extremely tired. The air pressure from flying seemed to be pulling on my womb. By the time I arrived home, it was only a few short hours until I started to spot and bleed. It wasn't much, but it alarmed Harry and me.

We called the doctor and went in to see him. He told us that I had probably already lost this baby, and even if we hadn't, it would only be a matter of days. My inner man was screaming, "No!" at the top of my lungs, but I forced myself to be calm on the outside. I told Harry I just could not believe the report of the doctor, and I would not lose this baby. We stood our ground together in the spirit realm for this baby. It certainly would have been great if an "angelic appearance" had occurred during this time, but it didn't.

You see, the angels are "seen" when the Father God wills it. We can't do anything to make it happen or not make it happen. We can't pray to them, worship them, give them orders, hold a crystal to get them to appear, or anything else. They are the servants of the Most High God, sent to help us accomplish our missions on the earth—that's all! They are not "gods" in any form, as some people have been misled to believe.

The week passed and Harry and I prayed, believed, confessed, and generally did everything we knew to do in faith. We didn't doubt. We didn't waver. But on Thursday night when I got out of bed and went into the bathroom, I passed out of my body what I recognized to be the flesh of our baby.

At that precise moment, I knew our baby boy's spirit passed right through my flesh and into the arms of his guardian angel. I was devastated! I didn't know what to do or say. I didn't know how to pray so I just sat there, numb from the pain in my heart and confused in my mind. The mother in me was grasping for the baby that I would not hold, that I would not rear, that I would not nurture.

Within a matter of seconds, God allowed me to see a precious vision that brought peace to my heart, my spirit, and my mind. I saw in my spirit that our baby, Malachi Charles, was escorted by his guardian angel to the throne room and into the presence of our Father God. *"And it occurred that the man [reduced to] begging died and was carried by the angels to Abraham's bosom..."* (Luke 16:22).

God allowed me to see our baby, forever in the presence of the Father God, waiting for us, his family, left on the earth. God gave me peace that someone would take care of him and nurture him just as I would have if he had stayed on the earth. Whether it be angels or saints who teach him about Jesus, I really don't care. Just as long as I know someone is teaching Malachi Charles to worship and to serve God with all of his heart, his mind, and his soul. Now my mother's heart can relax and rest in God.

That is not to say we didn't grieve. We were extremely sad and, yes, we grieved. But God healed our hearts and delivered us from our grief as He poured out His mercy upon us and gave us the grace to walk through the valley. Harry and I pulled together and poured the balm of healing from the Holy Spirit over each other's wounds until we could face the world again. It is so wonderful when you know you can rely on your "one flesh" (precious spouse) to help your wounded flesh and spirit.

Did we lose a battle? In the world's eyes it may seem as though we lost a battle, but in God's eyes we know we have won a greater victory. This is only temporary, only a separation; our Jesus has defeated death, and in Heaven there will be no more sorrow or death. We know where Malachi Charles is, and we know we will join him there some day soon.

> *Because we know that Christ (the Anointed One), being once raised from the dead, will never die again; death no longer has power over Him* (Romans 6:9).

> *God will wipe away every tear from their eyes; and death shall be no more, neither shall there be anguish (sorrow and mourning) nor grief nor pain any more, for the old conditions and the former order of things have passed away* (Revelation 21:4).

# 5

# ANGELS CAN TALK!

"Now angels talk! You're getting out there again, girl!" Wouldn't that be a normal response? I think so. But it wasn't mine. When Cheryl told me the angel talked to her, I believed her without question. Why? Because I believe in Cheryl and her unquestionable integrity. Everything Cheryl has done in her life up to now has been done with and by her tremendous faith in God. So why should I doubt her now? It wouldn't be consistent.

While producing a television show, I heard a guest, Rev. E.V. Hill from Los Angeles, California, clearly validate a man's ministry and life when many people were questioning that man's integrity. Rev. Hill told of the many miracles and achievements this man had seen and been a part of with God through nearly 70 years, laying them out in a convincing pattern that proved this man and what he said about the Gospel was true and real. Rev. Hill concluded by explaining that if everything up to this point was consistent and proved out, then believers should believe in the man of God and not what the world (or news media) wants them to believe about the man. He said to look for the consistency in the man's life and walk with God. I'll let Cheryl tell you what the angel said.

— *Harry Salem II*

In the fall of 1992, we were ministering in New Orleans. The service had begun with incredible music, worship, and praise. I began looking for the angels the minute we entered the building. I didn't see them even though I thought I could feel their peaceful presence.

The worshipers were ministering, and it was a pretty upbeat song. When they finished, two of the singers were very moved by the Holy Spirit and began to improvise their praise to the Father God. It began with beautiful back-and-forth singing between the two of them. It developed into the most gorgeous, uninhibited example of intimacy between the Father God and His children that I have ever seen. The two singers were operating in total freedom in the Father, completely surrendering their personhood, and the result was purity in praise. It was music, it was song, it was dance, it was God!

Right in the middle of this intimate display of worship, I felt the presence of the angels and looked up. There they were coming in by the hundreds! They took their stances around the top of the sanctuary, shoulder to shoulder, like warriors lining up for battle.

Weapons were drawn, eyes were searching for the enemy, and I could tell tonight was going to be another remarkable night in the spirit realm.

The service continued. I was sitting on the platform like I always do, but this platform was set up a little differently. Several pastors from various churches were seated on the platform in the second row behind me. I had my Bible open on my lap and was looking up the Scripture reference that had just been given. I felt someone tap me on the shoulder very firmly, and I assumed a pastor had missed the reference and needed to know what had been said. So I turned around expecting to see the face of a pastor. Instead, I was looking at the knees of the biggest angel I have ever seen! I looked up into his face, and he said in a very deep and authoritative voice, "Write this down!" It reminded me of the Scripture in Revelation 1:10-11, where John says:

> I was in the Spirit [rapt in His power] on the Lord's Day, and I heard behind me a great voice like the calling of a war trumpet, saying, "I am the Alpha and the Omega, the First and the Last. Write promptly what you see (your vision) in a book and send it...."

Of course, at a time like this, the only thing I had to write on was a tissue, and I couldn't find anything to write with! I scrounged through my Bible and finally found my pen and a piece of scratch paper.

Then this big angel actually spoke to me. I wrote like a mad woman, trying not to miss anything he said or how he said it. He said, "You have often wondered why we appear at different times in the service. We are released to come in when the praise becomes pure. Not when *you* think it is pure, but when God knows it is pure by the hearts of the people. Then we are allowed to come in and do our jobs."

I expected him to continue so I listened very carefully, but he said nothing more. I turned to look at him in anticipation of more, but he rose up to the ceiling and took his position back in the ranks of the other angels. I asked the Father God what the angel meant by "pure" praise.

The Holy Spirit revealed to me that so many times we think the praise is right when we have a certain feeling. But God said He examines the hearts of the people. He looks for unity in the hearts of the people. When there is unified praise without judgment between members of the Body, then His power is released. This releases the angels to come into the service with our miracles. This unified praise also releases the angels' ability to protect the miracles until we have had an opportunity to release our faith and receive our miracle.

What a service we had that evening! When the flow of the Holy Spirit began with the word of knowledge, I could have walked out in the crowd and told you who each one was with that particular need!

The word of knowledge is one of the spiritual gifts given by the Holy Spirit:

> To one is given in and through the [Holy] Spirit [the power to speak] a message of wisdom, and to another [the power to express] a word of knowledge and understanding according to the same [Holy] Spirit (I Corinthians 12:8).

It flows through people as a gift from God. The person being used by God with this gift may feel or see in the spirit God doing something (a healing miracle) in someone else's life. For example, a person operating in the gift of the word of knowledge may suddenly have a pain in his back, and immediately his mind will be enlightened as to what that pain is. As he says it out loud to the crowd, a person (or persons) having the trouble can then identify with it and believe God to heal him or her.

Sometimes, through the word of knowledge, I have seen the person, I know if it is a male or female, sometimes even know what the person is wearing, or know the person's name. God cannot be put in a box or be told how to do what He wants to do. No one can predict what He may do, or when, or even how. It is our job to be obedient to the voice of the Lord, have a willing heart, and trust God to use us.

How did I know who had a particular need? As a word of knowledge was given, an angel would leave the ranks of the others with a person's miracle in his hands, swoop down to that person in the audience, touch him or her, and then return to his original position. The angels moved so fast that it was impossible to see what they were holding, but I could see who they touched!

I was in astonishment and awe as person after person was touched by an angel with the miracle God had sent for each one. If I live to be 200 years old, I will never forget how I felt watching that miraculous interchange of faith and miracles! Faith literally took on the form of a substance in the supernatural realm. As faith was released to God, a type of exchange occurred. Faith was released and a miracle was received! And that night I watched in wonder as the angels brought God's healing gifts (miracles) to His people.

# 6

## ANGELS CAN BRING GOD'S
## HEALING

Cheryl is a walking, talking witness of the power of God to heal in His own miraculous ways. It took months for God to build a new bone in Cheryl's leg, but He did it. Then for six years she walked with one leg almost 2 inches shorter than the other. Her second miracle happened in the blink of an eye at a healing service when God lengthened her short leg by almost 2 inches. Did He use His angels to bring Cheryl's healing? Maybe so, maybe not. But after hearing Cheryl describe what she saw at the New Orleans church service, I believe He may have used the angels! If you need healing, don't give up. God has a miracle for you too!

— *Harry Salem II*

What I witnessed that night in the New Orleans church ser-vice affected my life and thinking dramatically. Watching such an event made me think about the story of Daniel in the Bible. Now I believe more than ever that too many people give up right before the angel gets to them with their answer.

The Scripture in Daniel 10 talks about the angel who tried to get to Daniel for quite a long time. However, the angel had been detained for 21 earthly days because he had to fight his way through the forces of evil (the prince of Persia). I believe that so many people's miracles are on their way. But the demonic forces have been sent to prevent the supernatural from happening, and the angels just haven't gotten through yet!

> And [the angel] said to me, O Daniel, you greatly beloved man, understand the words that I speak to you and stand upright, for to you I am now sent. And while he was saying this word to me, I stood up trembling. Then he said to me, Fear not, Daniel, for from the first day that you set your mind and heart to understand and to humble yourself before your God, your words were heard, and I have come as a consequence of [and in response] to your words. But the prince of the kingdom of Persia withstood me for twenty-one days. Then Michael, one of the chief [of the celestial] princes, came to help me, for I remained there with the kings of Persia (Daniel 10:11-13).

If we would just continue to believe, pray, and stand our ground in faith, I believe the miracle could eventually break through to us—just like Daniel's did. God says so plainly that when we ask, He answers. Then why are we not always receiving? Time, space, and assigned demonic assassins are all trying to stop what has already been done for us. That's where faith kicks in and says, "I will practice every fruit of the Spirit in my life. I will walk in love, joy, peace, patience, kindness, goodness, faithfulness, gentleness, and self-control. I will not stop believing my Father God who loves me. I know His Word, and I walk in the truth that has been given to set me free and keep me free!"

> *But the fruit of the [Holy] Spirit [the work which His presence within accomplishes] is love, joy (gladness), peace, patience (an even temper, forbearance), kindness, goodness (benevolence), faithfulness, gentleness (meekness, humility), self-control (self-restraint, continence). Against such things there is no law [that can bring a charge]* (Galatians 5:22-23).

Your answer *is* on its way! Don't quit! It's too soon to give up! Stay with your faith until your miracle arrives. It's not that your faith is weak or that you are being punished. We have to remember that the devil is still alive and well. He cannot defeat us, but he can harass us and cause distractions and troubles. During these times it's easy to get tired of waiting. Just realize that what you are asking God for has already been given. It is en route to you! Don't stop just short of receiving your miracle!

When I began to see the angels in the services in 1992, one of the most profound truths the Holy Spirit revealed to me was at the Buffalo, New York, service. I asked the Father God why the angels were there. He spoke to my heart and said they were there to protect the miracles.

That protection of the miracles was so evident to me at the New Orleans church. If you could have seen the angels, you would have known they were well capable of protecting the miracles! As the demonic forces tried to enter the room to stop the flow of the Holy Spirit, the angels fought to push them back outside the building and away from God's people. While some angels fought to hold back the demonic forces, others would leave the ranks to deliver miracles to God's people. There was such order and ease in the angels' strategy. If they were not fighting the demons or delivering a miracle, they would fall into formation with their arms crossed in front of their chests, standing at attention, shoulder to shoulder.

When the service began to come to a close, the miracles began to flow to the people in waves of anointing. There were so many miracles of healing that night! As I watched the undeniably divine orchestration of God, I was convinced that no *man* can start the move of God and no *man* can stop the move of God. All we can do is purify ourselves and humble ourselves and pray—giving God the praise and glory due His name.

The Scriptures teach that angels are involved in healing.

> *For an angel went down at a certain time into the pool and stirred up the water; then whoever stepped in first, after the stirring of the water, was made well of whatever disease he had* (John 5:4 NKJV).

You see, the angel brought the miracle to the pool, and the first one who stepped into the water received God's healing.

Sometimes healing is manifested quickly and other times years may pass. I don't know what the angel had to fight through to get God's best to me. One thing I do know: God is for me, not against me. Who could then eternally oppose me? I guess we have never given much thought as to how the miracle gets to us. I believe the angels bring the miracles to the earth. Maybe not every time, but certainly some of the times.

*"Bless the Lord, O my soul, and forget not all His benefits: Who forgives all your iniquities, who heals all your diseases"* (Psalm 103:2-3 NKJV).

Healing is one of God's benefits. And the angels are one of His benefits. Salvation is one of His benefits. Deliverance is one of His benefits. Peace is one of His benefits. Patience is one of His benefits. There are thousands of benefits listed in His Word. They are gifts freely given, always available to us.

Have we tapped into His tree with our branch and received all of His benefits for life? Dive into God's Word and begin today to receive His benefits in your life. And don't give up when things get tough—your angel is on its way with your miracle in tow.

# 7

# ANGELS IN WASHINGTON, DC

Where better to see warrior angels in battle than
Washington, DC, the most powerful city in the
world—a city that was designed by our forefathers
to intimidate all foreign heads of state who came
to deal with America and the American way of
life. But it didn't intimidate God or Cheryl when it
came to God's power.

— *Harry Salem II*

As a motivational speaker/minister, I sometimes work for several different secular organizations. They have me come in and share my "losing/winning" stories during Friday and Saturday night rallies. Many of these organizations provide a worship service on Sunday morning for those who desire to attend. At these Sunday worship services, I give my testimony and help with the altar service.

It was July 1982 in Washington, DC, at the Sheraton Hotel. There were about 6,000 in attendance on a Sunday morning—and the weekend had gone beautifully. I had shared my pageant story of overcoming years of losing, my healing testimony of surviving the devastating car wreck, and God had taken control of this meeting. I could just feel the presence of the Lord in the convention hall. Everyone else could feel it, too. There is something extremely exciting about God's anointing. It permeates the air you breathe, the seat you sit on, the floor you stand on. It permeates you—your very being.

I began flowing in the power of the Holy Spirit. I had submitted myself to the Scripture, Luke 12:12, that says, *"For the Holy Spirit will teach you in that very hour what you ought to say"* (NKJV). And the Holy Spirit was definitely directing my speaking!

A huge crowd of people had come forward for salvation. At least 3,000 people had either given their lives to the Lord for the first time or had rededicated their lives to Him. The word of knowledge began to flow, and I began to call out healings the Lord gave me through the Holy Spirit. God was touching people and healing them, saving them, drawing them to Him.

As I was ministering, I looked up at the mass of people surrounding the front of the platform, and something caught my eye. In the top of the room were thousands of angels! They must have been warrior angels because they were fighting with demonic forces that were also in the room and visible to my eyes. This was the first time I had seen angels and demons together engaged in combat.

The angels were fighting offensively, and the demons were fleeing out through the ceiling and the walls. The angels would then take a type of military stand, and the demons would begin to try and sneak back in! I could actually see them engage in battle. It was very distracting! Here I was trying to concentrate on what I was supposed to be doing, and an entire army of warriors was engaged in battle just above our heads!

The angels looked very much as I described them earlier. The demons had actual shape and form similar to the angels (head and body) and yet not like them at all. The demons were somewhat smaller than the angels. They were hideous in appearance. Ugly is not nearly a strong enough word to describe what they looked like.

They were gnarled, disfigured, slimy, creatures with horrible-looking tendrils or extensions that looked like some sort of roots in place of arms and hands. They looked bent over, crippled, and deformed. They seemed to be drooling some insidiously gross, green, slimy mess out of their mouths and literally out of their beings! They acted devious, sneaky, and cunning. Don't let their size fool you. They were not to be trusted. They were sent to destroy, and destroy they would do if given any opportunity at all!

I continued ministering, though I really don't know how I did. God was healing people all over the auditorium, and it seemed He was just beginning! The healing power and presence of God flowed like a gentle stream over the people. God was meeting each person at his or her own point of need. His anointing was breaking the yoke of bondage in peoples' lives—some were being healed physically, some were being delivered from emotional needs (such as abuse, fear, or addictions).

*It shall come to pass in that day that his burden will be taken away from your shoulder, and his yoke from your neck, and the yoke will be destroyed because of the anointing oil* (Isaiah 10:27 NKJV).

Some people were receiving Christ as their personal Savior, and many were recommitting themselves to Jesus. There was no doubt to those present that God was touching the hearts of these people in a most glorious way as testimony after testimony was given. The more testimonies that were shared, the more God moved among the people. The presence of the Lord in that place was absolutely undeniable.

You can imagine the impact that meeting had on my life. From that day forth, I began to hunger and thirst for more knowledge of the angelic realm. (Little did I know it would be ten years later in the summer of 1992 that the Lord would reveal the angels to me in an even greater magnitude and splendor.) I wanted to know why I had seen them, why their presence obviously brought about a tremendous breakthrough in the dimension of the Spirit, and how I could make sure they were in every one of the meetings where I was privileged to minister. God began to show me that it wasn't the presence of the angels that I was to seek after, but I was to seek after Him, His anointing, His presence. Then He would take care of everything else that was needed to accomplish His tasks through me. *"But seek first the kingdom of God and His righteousness, and all these things shall be added to you"* (Matt. 6:33 NKJV).

I was so excited to have seen the angels at a secular service. Yes, it was a Sunday worship service for the people in the organization, but obviously from the response of people being saved there were thousands of unsaved people present at that service. In Luke 15:10, Jesus says, *"...There is joy in the presence of the angels of God over one sinner who repents"* (NKJV). The angels were fighting and rejoicing to see people receive the goodness, love, and healing that God was pouring out to lead them to repentance.

> *Or do you despise the riches of His goodness, forbearance, and longsuffering, not knowing that the goodness of God leads you to repentance?* (Romans 2:4 NKJV)

Oh, the Father God loves us so much! And the angels rejoice when even one person receives the salvation that God has provided through Jesus! *"This is a faithful saying and worthy of all acceptance, that Christ Jesus came into the world to save sinners..."* (I Tim. 1:15 NKJV).

# 8

# LOOKING FOR THE REAL THING

If you think satan is going to just sit back and let God move on this earth and let His people see angels, then you need to pull open the drapes in your home and look outside. Lucifer (satan) was kicked out of Heaven because he wanted to be like God. Satan was the first counterfeit. In Isaiah 14:14, lucifer says, *"I will be like the Most High"* (NKJV). Now if he is reigning on this earth today (he is called *"the god of this world"* in Second Cor. 4:4), he must counterfeit what God is doing. Satan never ever had an original thought; he just perverts God's purity and goodness.

— *Harry Salem II*

It's easy to see why satan would try to counterfeit the true angels of God. The angels were created to bring God glory and have been provided as a benefit for us.

*Bless the Lord, you His angels, who excel in strength, who do His word, heeding the voice of His word. Bless the Lord, all you His hosts, you ministers of His, who do His pleasure* (Psalm 103:20-21 NKJV).

Satan doesn't want God glorified or us benefited! Everything that God creates for our benefit, satan will counterfeit and try to deceive us with it. The current "angel craze" is satan's counterfeit of the "real thing."

There are all kinds of books about angels on the market right now that are not backed by God's Word. They have a semblance of truth, and unless you are on your spiritual guard, even God's own people can be deceived and begin to receive into their spirits non-truths straight from satan himself. This could open you up to the demonic realm in full force and lead you down a destructive path. Satan's ploy is to deceive people into believing the "angels" they are communicating with are God's angels, when in fact they are demonic spirits masquerading as special messengers of God.

In these last days there will be many counterfeits sent from satan to confuse and mislead people—to take them away from God's best.

*And it is no wonder, for Satan himself masquerades as an angel of light; so it is not surprising if his servants also masquerade as ministers of righteousness. [But] their end will correspond with their deeds* (2 Corinthians 11:14-15).

We must know God's Word and the truth about His angels to protect ourselves and our families from deception. I believe this is why I have seen the angels and why God has allowed me the opportunity to share these occasions with you.

It takes knowing God's Word and listening to the voice of the Holy Spirit to be able to discern between the original (God's angels) and the counterfeit (satan's fallen angels). Thank the Father for the gift of discernment of spirits that helps us detect the realm of the spirits and their activities.[1] That is why the more encounters with the supernatural that I have had, the more studying, praying, and seeking God I have done.

> *But the manifestation of the Spirit is given to each one for the profit of all...to another discerning of spirits....But one and the same Spirit works all these things, distributing to each one individually as He wills* (1 Corinthians 12:7,10-11 NKJV).

There have been all kinds of speculations about the spiritual realm from just about everyone. Theologians, pastors, and evangelists have taught, studied, and written papers, books, and almost anything else you can think of on the subject of angels and demons. All of us are interested in the supernatural realm. We can't deny it. We can't stick our heads in the sand and hope it goes away. It won't. The biggest problem with sticking our heads in the sand is that generally our "other end" is sticking up in the air just begging someone to come along and kick us in the seat!

It is also evident that the people of the "world" (non-Christians) are very hungry for the supernatural realm. Psychics, psychic televison channels, and 1-900 telephone numbers to psychics have become big business, big entertainment, and big money in our country today. A lost world is looking for the truth in all the wrong places.

Many misguided individuals are attempting to contact the spirit realm through crystals or conjuring up angels. They are endeavoring through forms of yoga or mind-control meditation to "relax into a greater spiritual state." They are searching for answers, feelings, anything that will help them fill the void that only Jesus Christ can fill in their lives. They are hungry for the supernatural, and the devil has been filling that hunger. Because we are created as spirit beings (in a fleshly body), our spirit man cries out for its Creator—God Almighty. Therefore, people are going to reach out to the things of the supernatural. It is our responsibility to help them reach out and find truth, not deception.

Satan would love to completely deceive all people, both Christians and non-Christians. He does his best to steal from, kill, and destroy God's people wherever he can and to present counterfeits to the world about the supernatural realm. He would love for us to accept his lies and believe that we can conjure up our angels, that we can use crystals to help make us more spiritual, and many other ridiculous lies sent from the pit of hell to keep us from the truth of God.

We have the answers for the world's cry right in our Bibles. Yet we, and I am referring to God's children, are so afraid of what we may find that we pretend that it doesn't exist. It does exist, and people are going to seek out the spirit realm one way or the other.

I don't think we, as Christians, have realized the magnitude of our fearful, apathetic attitudes toward the supernatural realm or the impact of our attitudes on the souls of so many people who are hungry for the truth. It's our responsibility to know the truth. We must study, dig, discipline ourselves, pray, and seek to find the truth so we can share it with this dying world!

I want to share an experience with the supernatural realm I had in 1975 while I was a student at Mississippi State University. One evening Pam Williams, my wonderful Christian roommate, and I were reading the Word like we did every night before we went to bed. We turned the lights off and prayed for a while. After a short period of prayer, we were lying in our beds, supposably going to sleep. I just couldn't sleep. Something just was not right. I felt a strange uneasiness, a disturbance or restlessness in my thinking.

I was lying there with my eyes open, just emptily gazing at the ceiling, when suddenly I saw a black cloud of the darkest darkness begin to pour into the ceiling of the room. It moved like smoke or fog and yet it had a type of form, too dense to be a vapor. It filled the entire ceiling, and it was immediately evident to my spirit that this was an evil presence—a demonic spirit sent from the pit of hell.

Instantly, I was gripped with fear. I tried to say something to Pam, but because I was so afraid, I couldn't get the words out. I finally squeaked out a petrified, "P—P—Pam!" She whispered, "Jesus!" She was seeing the demonic presence, too. As Pam said the name of Jesus, I jumped off my bed and onto Pam's as quickly as possible. Somehow her bed just seemed safer at the time!

We immediately began praying. We were so scared that all we could really say was "Jesus, Jesus," over and over. We both began to call upon the power of the Holy Spirit to pray with us. When we don't know what to pray, or we are too scared to think, the Holy Spirit who dwells in us can take over and pray for us. He knows at all times what is needed to be effective in the war against the enemy.

> So too the [Holy] Spirit comes to our aid and bears us up in our weakness; for we do not know what prayer to offer nor how to offer it worthily as we ought, but the Spirit Himself goes to meet our supplication and pleads in our behalf with unspeakable

*yearnings and groanings too deep for utterance. And He Who
searches the hearts of men knows what is in the mind of the
[Holy] Spirit [what His intent is], because the Spirit intercedes
and pleads [before God] in behalf of the saints according to and
in harmony with God's will* (Romans 8:26-27).

As we prayed, the dark, vile cloud began to dissipate. This
took several hours! It wasn't just "poof" and it was gone. Even
though the evil presence's power was paralyzed and disarmed
instantly when we spoke the name of Jesus, it took several hours
for us to make our stand. It took constant dedication to prayer and
a constant stance in battle to eliminate fear from our minds before
it left completely. James 4:7 says, *"Submit to God. Resist the devil and
he will flee from you"* (NKJV). It took consistent prayer action in
submission to God to steadily push back that demonic force to
make it leave us.

When we felt it had sufficiently been defeated, I got off Pam's
bed and made my way to the door where the light switch was
located. I felt like a nice, bright light might be very helpful at this
point! As I approached the door, I noticed a small, dark cloud on
the floor right by the door about 2 feet in diameter. It was too late
to turn back now. I was already almost on top of it. So I reached
out (in faith and this time not afraid) and flipped on the light. The
cloud immediately left!

I realize now the difference in my attitude toward that last
remaining "spot" on the floor and the large cloud in the ceiling
was the time we had just spent in prayer. The prayer time had
allowed me to fellowship with my Father God—my faith had been
built, thus dissipating the fear.

Pam and I spent most of the night reading the Word, studying, and praying. We sought God's face and direction in this matter. As we prayed, God began to reveal to us that we were embarking into spiritual warfare, and we needed to be prepared to battle satan and his demons from this day forward. We were leading people out of darkness (satan's domain) into the glorious light of Jesus through salvation. Satan and his little demons were not going to give up without a fight.

In so many ways it seems like this just happened yesterday. I will never forget how scared I was. I can't express how strongly I thought that satan had come to literally kill Pam and me. I had never experienced the feeling of fear like that before—I never have been one to be afraid. Yet I believe God allowed the incident to open both Pam's and my eyes to the reality of the supernatural realm. I believe satan wanted to kill us and stop us from witnessing about Jesus.

The first lesson I learned was that satan cannot kill me. I know he can't because if he could he would have already done so. He may try to scare me to death, but he can't do that, either. He may even try to make you think that he is going to kill you, but if he can't make you believe that he is going to kill you, then he can't do it! Remember, satan's whole strategy is deception. He cannot take anything from us that we do not give him. He wants to get us operating in fear instead of faith.

Fear is satan's "faith." It is the perversion or counterfeit of God's faith. Picture a coin. You have faith on one side and fear on the other. We either operate in faith, or we operate in fear. That is why satan is so determined to get you into fear—because if he can get you operating in fear, you won't be operating in faith.

Fear will literally paralyze you and keep you from fulfilling God's purpose and destiny for you on this earth. If we can recognize  satan's strategy, we can choose not to fear. We may "feel" fear, but we can choose not to *react or respond in fear*. We can watch our mouths (not constantly saying, "I'm so afraid!" etc.), and we can call upon the power of the Holy Spirit to help us walk in our God-given authority. God allowed me to learn a wonderfully powerful lesson that night with regards to fear. Remember, F-E-A-R could stand for False Evidence Appearing Real!

From that day on I have *never* been afraid of satan. I will never fear him or his little wimpy demons again. With the Word of God and the name of Jesus on our lips, satan can't harm us. This great revelation has helped me many nights when satan has tried to slip in and put fear in my heart. We never have to fear the demonic realm! Remember, only "one-third" of the angels fell and became followers of satan. That means God's army of angels outnumbers the demonic realm two to one!

The second lesson I learned was that the spirit realm, which includes demons and angels, is much closer than we think. The realm where the angels and demons move (the spirit realm) is a parallel realm (world) to the natural world in which we live and breathe. It exists even though we can't see it with our natural eyes. We can't see the air that we breathe, but we know and have faith that it is there.

The angels and the demons are in the spirit realm. This is why I have shared my college "demon" experience with you. It is extremely important that we have accurate knowledge according to God's Word before we start fighting something we know very little about.

A few years ago, Harry was on a crusade in California. Between services Harry and several of the men on the crusade team went to eat dinner. They finished dinner and were walking down the street when they saw an amusement center with miniature golf, batting cages, video games, etc. Behind these attractions were miniature Indianapolis-style race cars on display. So the men strolled into the building to look at these "wonderful" cars.

As they entered, Harry felt a dark presence in the building and felt the people there turning and staring at them. He immediately said to his friends, "Do you feel that?" His friends all said, "What? Feel what?" Harry answered, "It's a demonic presence, and we are not welcome here. We either need to leave or get ready for a fight." So they left and found out later that the people in that building were waiting for a heavy-metal rock concert to begin across the street. The demonic spirit was in the people, and it hated God's Spirit in Harry and the other men.

The best way to get defeated is to go into battle and know nothing about the enemy or how to utilize your own army. Don't run into the front lines of battle without your armor. Too many people, in their zeal for the Lord, have run out into warfare against the enemy with nothing more covering them than their pajamas, and they get shot up pretty badly. All the while they cry out to God, "Why are You letting this happen to me?" And always remember there are times to confront the enemy and other times to be led by the Spirit to leave like Harry and his friends did.

I am reminded of the Scripture in Ephesians 6:10-18. It reads so beautifully in the *Amplified Bible*:

*In conclusion, be strong in the Lord [be empowered through your union with Him]; draw your strength from Him [that strength which His boundless might provides].*

*Put on God's whole armor [the armor of a heavy-armed soldier which God supplies], that you may be able successfully to stand up against [all] the strategies and the deceits of the devil.*

*For we are not wrestling with flesh and blood [contending only with physical opponents], but against the despotisms, against the powers, against [the master spirits who are] the world rulers of this present darkness, against the spirit forces of wickedness in the heavenly (supernatural) sphere.*

*Therefore put on God's complete armor, that you may be able to resist and stand your ground on the evil day [of danger], and, having done all [the crisis demands], to stand [firmly in your place].*

*Stand therefore [hold your ground], having tightened the belt of truth around your loins and having put on the breastplate of integrity and of moral rectitude and right standing with God,*

*And having shod your feet in preparation [to face the enemy with the firm-footed stability, the promptness, and the readiness produced by the good news] of the Gospel of peace.*

*Lift up over all the [covering] shield of saving faith, upon which you can quench all the flaming missiles of the wicked [one].*

*And take the helmet of salvation and the sword that the Spirit wields, which is the Word of God.*

*Pray at all times (on every occasion, in every season) in the Spirit, with all [manner of] prayer and entreaty. To that end keep alert and watch with strong purpose and perseverance, interceding in behalf of all the saints (God's consecrated people).*

Get in the Word of God to gain knowledge and understanding of the war that is not against flesh and blood. Put on your armor and wield your sword (the Word of God). And through the power of the Holy Spirit, the intervention of the angels of God, the blood of the Lamb, and the word of your testimony you will overcome the enemy and be victorious in Jesus.

Many people tell me they are interested in the angelic realm. That's great! What I want you to understand is that you can't pick and choose who or what you see in that realm or even when you see in that realm. Demons are present and so are angels in the dimension of the spirit, so get prepared for war!

The point I am trying to make is that you may never see into that realm. Whether you see the angels or demons is totally beside the point. The real issue is that they do truly exist. You can deny their existence, but it won't make them go away.

When we, as Christians, become grounded in the truth that we have all authority over the demonic realm through the power of Jesus Christ of Nazareth, we won't walk in fear any longer. When we understand that God has provided the angels for our benefit as powerful warriors ready to do battle on our behalf, then we can truly go into all the world and preach the Gospel, the good news, for the earth and its inhabitants.

God has the truth and we know it. We can no longer sit in our "spiritual comfort zones" and let the world die of spiritual hunger around us. Remember, satan is seeking whom he "may" devour: *"Be sober, be vigilant; because your adversary the devil walks about like a roaring lion, seeking whom he may devour"* (I Pet. 5:8 NKJV).

What are we going to do about seeking the truth and sharing it with the world? I don't know about you, but I know I am finally willing to forget about my pride or what people may think and get in touch with God's truth about the spirit realm. I am ready to face the onslaught of the enemy, the ridicule of the Christian community, the skepticism and questions of argumentative so-called godly people, and take the answers that I have found in God's Word to a hungry and spiritually dying world.

So choose to read God's Word (Scriptures on angels are in the back of this book) and familiarize yourself with the truth. Listen to the voice of your heavenly Father God and trust the prompting of the Holy Spirit. Then pray as Solomon prayed, *"Give to Your servant an understanding heart to judge Your people, that I may discern between good and evil..."* (I Kings 3:9 NKJV).

## ENDNOTE

1. Jack W. Hayford, exec. ed., *Spirit-Filled Life Bible* (Nashville: Thomas Nelson, 1991), H.S. Gifts and Power; 2025, #7.

# 9

# THE REAL THING: ANGELS OF PROTECTION

Why not a big angel? Why not a protector? We serve a big God. Revelation 1:7 says, *"Behold, He is coming with clouds, and every eye will see Him, even they who pierced Him..."* (NKJV). This Scripture tells us we serve a big God. Now why would a big God send us a little angel? I am reminded of a man who once told me the only picture he had of Jesus was that of a long-haired guy in a white robe holding a sheep. And he said, "Why would I, a former biker, want to have that wimp as my Savior or Protector?" See how the images man creates can affect us? Let me tell you. My Savior was not a weak, wimpy guy with long hair wearing a robe. He was the most masculine, strong man who ever walked this earth. He bore all man's sickness and sin on the cross of Calvary and then died for us. He rose again three days later with the keys to hell and death in His hand. A big God. Yes—our Protector from before time began. So why not a big angel? A protector without a doubt!

— *Harry Salem II*

We need to know the truth about the angels from God's Word. And Psalm 103:20-21 helps us understand God's purpose for angels:

> *Bless the Lord, you His angels, who excel in strength, who do His word, heeding the voice of His word. Bless the Lord, all you His hosts, you ministers of His, who do His pleasure* (NKJV).

These verses show that angels exist to serve God in five ways: (1) to "bless the Lord" (in worship and service); (2) to "do His Word" (concerning activities on earth); (3) to heed the voice of God's Word (as it is spoken through the saints on earth); (4) to minister on God's behalf [as described in Hebrews 1:14: *"Are they not all ministering spirits sent forth to minister for those who will inherit salvation?"* (NKJV)]; and (5) to do God's pleasure (as His hosts are at His direction).[1] These verses provide a backdrop of God's truth about angels.

The angels also protect you. You can count on it! I am reminded of two powerful Scriptures God gives us. *"The angel of the Lord encamps all around those who fear Him, and delivers them"* (Psalm 34:7 NKJV). I definitely like the thought of God's angels encamping around me!

The other verse, the most quoted verse of protection when referring to angels, is Psalm 91:11-12: *"For He shall give His angels charge over you, to keep you in all your ways. In their hands they shall bear you up, lest you dash your foot against a stone"* (NKJV). Dr. Billy Graham, observing the plural in this text, concluded that each believer must have at least two angels whose assigned duty it is to protect them.[2] Dr Graham has a long-standing track record of his walk with God. I tend to think he is right that we have more than one guardian angel, at least in certain instances. One thing is certain: each of us has at least one as our own guardian angel! And the Lord graciously allowed me to see mine at a time when I needed assurance in my life. Let me relate the story of my first introduction to my guardian angel.

I had been in full-time ministry since the year I was Miss America. I was traveling, ministering, singing, preaching, and giving my testimony. Yet I found myself caught in the trap of silently searching for everyone's approval—including my Father God's. You may be thinking, *What's so bad about wanting God's approval? That doesn't sound like a bad thing.*

No, it doesn't sound wrong, but it is wrong when the motive behind your actions is to gain approval. God doesn't look upon our actions as much as He looks upon our hearts.

> *But the Lord said to Samuel, "Do not look at his appearance or at the height of his stature, because I have refused him. For the Lord does not see as man sees; for man looks at the outward appearance, but the Lord looks at the heart"* (1 Samuel 16:7 NKJV).

The things I was doing were good, and God was graciously bringing about great outcomes in other people's lives. Yet my own mind was crying out for someone to say that I was "OK"—I desperately wanted approval. God was allowing the dross to come to the top from childhood wounds of abuse that were causing me to feel rejection. And I had not come to grips with the fact that God had "already" accepted and approved me.

*And I will bring My hand again upon you and thoroughly purge away your dross [as with lye] and take away all your tin or alloy* (Isaiah 1:25).

God says in Second Corinthians 3:4-5 that we are not competent to claim anything for ourselves, but our competence comes from God.

*Such confidence as this is ours through Christ before God. Not that we are competent in ourselves to claim anything for ourselves, but our competence comes from God* (NIV).

I have God's competence! I have God's stamp of approval on me! I don't have to continually try and earn His approval. I do not have to "perform" in order for Him to love me. I have already been accepted in the Beloved! *"To the praise of the glory of His grace, wherein he hath made us accepted in the beloved"* (Eph. 1:6 KJV).

I am not saying that we shouldn't work hard for God. I am saying that the motive of the heart is very important to God. I've had to learn that God's love for me is unconditional. His love for me is not based on my performance, even in ministry for Him. Our motive must be genuine compassion and love for our fellow man. God is constantly looking for people with pure motives through whom He can pour His anointing to a lost and hurting world.

In 1984, I began traveling with a team of musicians instead of by myself, singing with tracks. I had been ministering alone for several years just using soundtracks and accompanying myself on the piano. I was going through a desert time where I was lonely. I wanted and needed people around me who loved and supported me. Like I said, I was not receiving the acceptance and love that the Father God longed to give me.

I have never been as miserable, before or since, as I was during that time. I just didn't want to be by myself. I was hurting on the inside and I was lonely. I had wounds from the past that had only been band-aided, never healed. I asked several musician friends, and my brother, Heath, if they would travel and minister with me for a while. We rented a bus, and instead of flying by myself to churches, we would drive, set up all the equipment, and have *live* music instead of taped.

All I have ever wanted to do is feel the presence of God on me and flowing through me. Just to know that He will use me for His glory has always been the cry of my heart. I wanted to minister and bring to others what God had allowed me to see and have from Him. I wanted others to get healed, saved, and delivered. And through the giving of myself for others' needs, I was believing God for my needs and hurts to be healed.

We were in Winter Park, Florida, at Calvary Assembly Church. Inside I was battling personal attacks, and my mind was a battlefield. I was dealing with terrible thoughts from within of inadequacy, fear of failure, no self-worth, fear of rejection, and pain. In spite of the turmoil within me, the anointing was strong upon me. That is the grace of our God.

I could feel the gentle presence of the Holy Spirit in the place. The more we sang His praises and the more I shared from my heart, the more of God's precious presence I could feel. As we were bringing the service to a close, I was singing "Holy Ground."

When I first recorded this song, the glory of God and His healing anointing was upon it even in the recording studio. The songwriter, whom I had never met before, had dropped this song in the mail to me. And from the first moment I heard him sing the chorus, "We are standing on holy ground, and I know that there are angels all around. Let us praise Jesus now, we are standing in His presence on holy ground," God's sweet anointing came pouring into my home, my heart, my life, my very being. I knew this song was for me to sing, and as I sang it, people would be healed and delivered from the demonic oppressive spirits that had been sent on assignment against them. I knew people would give their hearts to Jesus!

I hardly ever ministered without singing this song somewhere within the service, and this night in Winter Park was no different. As I sang, the presence of God literally enveloped the room. The anointing was so strong I could feel it with my hands. When I got to the line in the song, "and there are angels all around," I gestured all around the entire upper half of the auditorium, sweeping my hand in a circular motion from my left shoulder very slowly all the way around to my right shoulder. As I turned my head and eyes to follow my hand over my right shoulder, there stood an incredibly big angel! I'm sure my eyes went wide—I was shocked to see him there! He had to be at least 12 feet tall!

This big angel was massive, gorgeous, and powerful looking. His arms, chest, and legs were rippling with muscles. He was wearing loose-fitting pants that came just below his knees and a type of opened-front vest that revealed his chest and arms. He was beautifully proportioned in his form and had the most serious look on his face. His hair was about shoulder length, and his eyes were like looking into deep pools of pure love. The angel seemed to command attention from within himself and designated service to his Creator as the utmost of importance.

He looked out over the crowd, as if he were surveying the movements of the crowd, and never seemed to notice me down below him. Now I realize the angel was watching for the onslaught of the enemy that was trying to kill, steal, and destroy me.

> *The thief does not come except to steal, and to kill, and to destroy. I have come that they may have life, and that they may have it more abundantly* (John 10:10 NKJV).

I don't know how I managed to keep singing. I continually turned around to see if the angel was still standing there. That's kind of a funny expression to say that he was "standing" there. His feet were not on the floor! They were way up in the air, but he was standing on the air!

I looked at the rest of the team to see if anyone else was seeing him. I knew I would be able to tell by the expression on their faces. My brother, Heath, was traveling with me that summer, singing backup and learning all he could about ministering. I saw the look on his face, and I knew he could see the angel, too.

After the service concluded, Heath came running up to me and excitedly said, "Did you see him? Cheryl, did you see him?" Of course I said that I did, and I was relieved that he could see him, too. There was only one difference. Heath couldn't see him after the service was over, but I still could.

The angel got on the bus and traveled to Washington, DC, with us. I know you are thinking, *You're kidding, right? He got on the bus? Why?* I don't know, I guess he wanted to ride! I shared this news with my ministry team; and, of course, they wanted to know what he was doing and where was he sitting. It almost became comical! They would ask about where he was sitting, and I would tell them, "Wherever he wants to!"—which was true! The angel sat (and stood and sat and stood) in front of me and always kept a vigilant eye scanning all directions around me.

You see, the spiritual realm in which I was being allowed to see is parallel to the realm we call the natural world. It looks like it, with a few exceptions. I was seeing both realms at the same time, almost like looking into the layers of a color separation of a photograph. Most of the time we see almost all the layers of the picture but not quite. At that moment, I was being allowed to see the final layer of the picture. So the angel sat wherever he wanted to, because we (humans) were not in his realm. We weren't in the last layer of the picture. Does that make sense to you?

When we checked into the hotel, the angel got off the bus and went in the hotel room with me. I was feeling very awkward and uncomfortable about all of this now! Not that I didn't enjoy him, but he wasn't saying a word. He wasn't doing anything except look-ing—he was just there. Why was he hanging around?

Did he have something to tell me? I tried to talk to him, but he just stood there with his arms folded across that massive chest and looked around the room. I finally asked the Father God why he was here. The Holy Spirit spoke in my heart and told me he was my guardian angel, and he was there to protect me. The Holy Spirit told me his name is Gabion, and He even spelled it for me! He said that *Gabion* means "protector," and I was his assignment and had been all of my life.

What a revelation! I can't tell you how I felt at that moment. It was as if God Himself gave me assurance that He had His hand upon me, and He would never leave me or forsake me. I needed that very message so badly!

From that day on, I have never felt alone or lonely again. I know that no matter how bad things may look, God has His hand on me. I believe that God probably assigned my guardian angel to me *even before* I was born because Jeremiah 1:5 says, *"Before I formed you in the womb I knew you; before you were born I sanctified you..."* (NKJV). My guardian angel was probably there when I was in my mother's womb!

Gabion's presence was manifested to me for three days and nights. After that, I couldn't see him any longer, but I knew that he was there, doing his job, protecting me and the call placed upon my life.

Praise God we, as Christians, all have angels to protect us! As we have seen in Hebrews 1:14, *"ministering spirits...minister for those who will inherit salvation"* (NKJV).

Psalm 91 includes a great promise about angels, but notice the way in which this passage begins:

> *Because you have made the Lord, who is my refuge, even the Most High, your dwelling place, no evil shall befall you, nor shall any plague come near your dwelling; for He shall give His angels charge over you, to keep you in all your ways. In their hands they shall bear you up, lest you dash your foot against a stone. You shall tread upon the lion and the cobra, the young lion and the serpent you shall trample underfoot* (Psalm 91:9-13 NKJV).

We must abide in the Lord and His Word to qualify for angelic protection from the Father God.

I have learned to pray Psalm 91 in its entirety over my family and me. If you do not do this already, you may want to incorporate this prayer over your family. Personalize it by putting the Scripture in first person, *I, me, my,* etc., as you pray. It is very important to understand this and to say to yourself, "The Word of God is written for my benefit, not against me, *but for me!*" Psalm 103:2 encourages us not to forget even one of God's benefits. The angels are a benefit sent for protection from the Father God. *"Bless the Lord, O my soul, and forget not all His benefits"* (Ps. 103:2 NKJV).

Every time I pray Psalm 91 over my family, friends, or myself, I think of Gabion. I have seen Gabion on two other occasions since the initial three-day incident.

On both occasions, during two different women's conferences, we were in an evening service and the praise was magnificent. You could feel the attentive presence of the Holy Spirit and knew that God was present to meet the needs of His women.

The first time I rather abruptly felt the awesome presence of the angels. I looked around the ceiling, where I had become accustomed to look for them, and there he was! All I could see was one mighty angel, but he was one I recognized. In the back of the ballroom, over my right shoulder, Gabion was standing in that now familiar stance. With the light of the Father shining through him, his countenance brought instant peace to my soul.

He was looking all around but not at me. I was used to his manner of protection and knew it was for my good. I was so glad to see him there to protect the meeting and to protect me. I realized then, even as I do now, that it was not my seeing him that brought about his protection. He was there doing his job all along. Whether I ever see him again or not does not change the fact that he is always with me, ever protecting me from the adversary.

On the other occasion I was privileged to have my spiritual eyes opened, and I saw Gabion again. The circumstances were the same, he looked and acted the same, and he did his job. It never ceases to inspire me that God is ever protecting me and watching over my life.

Yes, God has allowed me to literally "see" my guardian angel, but that makes it no more real for me than for you. Your guardian angel, assigned by the Father God, is there on your behalf too. Seeing the angels is a serendipity (an unexpected surprise) from the Father God, but your victory will come from constant and consistent abiding in the Father, His Word, and His presence.

## ENDNOTES

1. Jack W. Hayford, exec. ed., *Spirit-Filled Life Bible* (Nashville: Thomas Nelson, 1991), Kingdom, 842.

2. Billy Graham, *Angels* (Nashville: Thomas Nelson, 1995).

3. *Spirit-Filled Life Bible*, Kingdom, 833.

# 10

# "Gabion"—Do Angels Have Names?

I've never seen my guardian angel, but, in faith, I believe he is with me all the time. Does he have a name? I trust the Lord picked one that is significant. You'll just have to trust the Bible on this issue. It explains it better than I ever could, and it's more convincing, too!

— *Harry Salem II*

Just as the Holy Spirit told me my guardian angel's name is "Gabion," spelled it for me, and then told me it means "my protector," I believe all the angels have different names. God's Word gives us the names of three different angels—Gabriel (God's messenger), Michael (chief or archangel), and lucifer (fallen angel now called satan). According to my studies, these are the only names of angels that are revealed to us through His Word. However, it is easy to surmise that names are extremely significant to God.

From the earliest times, the name given to a child was supposed to indicate some characteristic of the person; of the circumstances, trivial or momentous, connected with his or her birth; of the hopes, beliefs, or feelings of the parents. This is evident from the etymologies found in the following Scriptures, which testify to the impression that names and facts should correspond:[1]

> And Abraham called the name of his son who was born to him—whom Sarah bore to him—Isaac. And Sarah said, "God has made me laugh, and all who hear will laugh with me" (Genesis 21:3,6 NKJV).

> And Esau said, "Is he not rightly named Jacob? For he has supplanted me these two times. He took away my birthright, and now look, he has taken away my blessing!" (Genesis 27:36 NKJV)

> And the child grew, and she brought him to Pharaoh's daughter, and he became her son. So she called his name Moses, saying, "Because I drew him out of the water" (Exodus 2:10 NKJV).

> Then she named the child Ichabod, saying, "The glory has departed from Israel!" because the ark of God had been captured and because of her father-in-law and her husband (I Samuel 4:21 NKJV).

> Please, let not my lord regard this scoundrel Nabal. For as his name is, so is he: Nabal is his name, and folly is with him! (I Samuel 25:25 NKJV).

Each name given by God throughout His Word had a significant meaning. The first record in the Word of God naming an unborn baby is in Genesis 16:11. Here the angel of the Lord is speaking to Hagar, the handmaiden of Sarah, who was pregnant with Abraham's firstborn son. The angel tells Hagar to name the baby *Ishmael*, which means "God hears."

> *And the Angel of the Lord continued, "See now, you are with child and shall bear a son, and shall call his name Ishmael [God hears], because the Lord has heard and paid attention to your affliction"* (Genesis 16:11).

In Luke 1:13 we read of another angel speaking to the father of an unborn baby.

> *But the angel said to him, "Do not be afraid, Zachariah, because your petition was heard, and your wife Elizabeth will bear you a son, and you must call his name John" [God is favorable].*

This baby was, of course, John the Baptist. The name of an individual was in a sense a prophecy or destiny of the person.

God certainly named our precious Savior with absolute significance. An angel gave Mary the name of the Messiah to be born; *"...and you shall call His name Jesus"* (Luke 1:31). *Jesus* means "God with us." These names were all synonymous with the definitions and callings of the persons to which they were given. To me it just stands to reason then that the names of the angels would be consistent with this philosophy.

Just because we may not know the names of each angel doesn't mean they don't have names. When you go to eat in a restaurant, you may not know the name of everyone who is present, but they all have names. I believe all angels have names, too.

The angel in many cases who is referred to as "God's angel" or "My angel" is named Gabriel. Luke 1:19 says, *"I am Gabriel, who stands in the presence of God"* (NKJV). This gives me the impression that Gabriel is a special angel to God. *Gabriel* means "God's messenger" and "mighty one of God"—so the very name implies a special position.

Another angel named in the Bible is Michael, whose name means "chief" or "archangel." Daniel 10:13 refers to Michael:

> *But the prince of the kingdom of Persia withstood me twenty-one days; and behold, Michael, one of the chief princes, came to help me, for I had been left alone there with the kings of Persia* (NKJV).

Lucifer was one of God's angels before he fell from Heaven. Lucifer fell because he wanted to be like God and tried to usurp God's authority. The name *lucifer* means "beautiful one."

> *How you are fallen from heaven, O Lucifer, son of the morning! For you have said in your heart: "I will ascend into heaven, I will exalt my throne above the stars of God; I will also sit on the mount of the congregation on the farthest sides of the north; I will ascend above the heights of the clouds, I will be like the Most High"* (Isaiah 14:12-14 NKJV).

Before the Fall, lucifer was the most beautiful angel in Heaven, according to Ezekiel 28:12: *"...You were the seal of perfection, full of wisdom and perfect in beauty"* (NKJV). When you read this entire chapter of Ezekiel, you may notice that lucifer had musical "parts" within him. Ezekiel 28:13 reads, *"...The workmanship of thy tabrets and of thy pipes was prepared in thee in the day that thou wast created"* (KJV).

The Hebrew word for "tabrets" is *toph*, which means a tambourine or timbrel.[2] Satan or lucifer had within himself the ability of music. In Ezekiel 28:13 the musical reference suggests that satan's role included leading Heaven's choirs in the worship of the Most High.[3] I believe, because of his workmanship, lucifer was the archangel of praise and worship.

We must remember that all things are created for God and His good pleasure. I believe God created music for His pleasure. Satan has tried to pervert music. I believe this is because he was once the one who worshiped God in the most gloriously beautiful music. Because satan fell from Heaven, music that glorifies God stings to the very core of his being. Therefore, satan has tried to destroy today's music, to ruin it, and to bring praise and glory to himself with perversion. Yes, satan has gotten into much of today's music and turned it against God. That is why God had to change lucifer's name (meaning "beautiful one") to satan (meaning "adversary" in the Hebrew or "accuser" in the Greek).

I'm sure all the angels have names and their names have meanings. When a friend of mine, Laura Jacobs, saw her angel, God told her the angel's name is *Iddo*, which means "festive." This totally fits Laura's personality! Her angel, Iddo, never spoke a word to her with his mouth, but his very presence exuded the words to her spirit, *Be not afraid.* She felt these words in her very being. She didn't need to hear them.

Laura has a beautiful relationship with the Father. She asked God to give her the names of her family's angels. The Holy Spirit spoke to her and told her that her husband's angel's name is *Sammon*, which means "watchman." Her two children's angels' names are *Abrion*, which means "Father exalted," and *Pharr*, which means "quicken or hasten."

Who knows what all the angels' names are? Only God! I'm sure they are all significant to us here on this earth whether we know their names or not!

## ENDNOTES

1. *Hastings Dictionary of the Bible* (Hendrickson Pub., 1989), 643.

2. Ibid., 889.

3. Jack W. Hayford, exec. ed., *Spirit-Filled Life Bible* (Nashville: Thomas Nelson, 1991), Commentary, 1195.

# II

## ARE THE ANGELS ALWAYS WITH US?

This chapter reminds me of the movie *It's a Wonderful Life* with Jimmy Stewart. This is where the "what if's" come into play. "What if I had never existed?" was the theme in this movie. We are the "what if" society. But we don't get the luxury of seeing "what if" something happened differently, like Jimmy Stewart did in the movie. Recently, when a friend's home was vandalized, he was so concerned about what had happened that he didn't consider what didn't happen. It could have been much worse. Now read how a "what if" type of experience touched our lives.

— *Harry Salem II*

I know that Gabion, my private guardian angel, is always with me even though I do not always see him. I know that my children's guardian angels are with them constantly even though the angels are not visible to my eyes. I must trust the Father God and His protection for my children and stand on His promise in Psalm 91:11 that He will give His angels charge over them to keep them in all their ways.

When Harry and I were opening our first retail store, we did most of the work ourselves. We painted, cleaned, wallpapered, scrubbed—we did everything! Come to think of it, maybe *Harry* did most of that stuff! Sorry, Honey, I'll try to do better next time!

Anyway, we were at the store getting everything together. Li'l Harry, who was four years old at the time, was with us. It was very hard for us to go anywhere without him! Harry and Li'l Harry were in the back room putting up racks and shelves. I was up front doing little odd jobs.

Li'l Harry is a very busy child and has always been a handful! He is also a climber. Well, this particular day he climbed up on a metal cabinet that was not yet attached to the wall. He pulled it over on himself with the loudest crash I have ever heard! It all happened in only a matter of seconds.

The cabinet was very heavy, and it came crushing down on his little body full force! He was completely pinned under the weight of it. Because the cabinet was metal, it cut across his face and blood was everywhere!

*Why did it have to be blood?* I thought. When I had been in the car wreck as a child, blood was everywhere. The minute I saw my own child's blood, I went right back in my mind to the place where I had been pinned in the car and covered with blood. *Not his face!*

my mind was screaming. Harry was very calm and took charge immediately. Thank God he did! I was a nervous wreck!

Harry told me to go call the doctor, and I took off running. The phone in our store was not hooked up yet, so I headed through the complex to find a phone and call Dr. Mike Ritze, our family physician, whose number I had memorized.

When I finally found a phone, I couldn't think of the number! I couldn't even think of my name or what I was doing! I was a mess! I finally calmed down enough to think of it, and Dr. Mike told us to meet him at his office immediately.

As we drove to the doctor's office, my mind was racing. *What did I do wrong? Why wasn't I back there with him? Why had I let him climb on everything? I'm a terrible mother. It's all my fault! Where were the angels that I assign every day in prayer over him?* I couldn't come up with answers to any of my questions.

My mind was like a tumultuous, emotional tornado ready to strike with full force! I was begging God to please keep my child from being scarred on his face. I had grown up with multiple scars on my face and didn't want my child to have to go through trauma of any kind, much less a tragedy similar to one from my childhood.

Miraculously, the injuries were relatively minor as far as the future was concerned. He looked absolutely horrible at the time with stitches in his face, under his nose, and right in the middle of his cheek. His eye had been hit with such force that the blood vessels were broken. He looked just awful, but it would heal without a trace of problem to the eye. He does have a scar under his nose and right across his cheek, but they aren't a detriment to his handsome looks!

By the time we got Li'l Harry home and settled down, I was beginning to get vocal with some of my questions, especially about the whereabouts of the angels! Dr. Mike had told us while he was stitching Li'l Harry up how this shelf should have done much worse damage to his face. He said the weight of it could have crushed Li'l Harry's chest, and his eye could have been put completely out!

After several days God finally got my attention. It took my precious husband, Harry, with his rational and logical mind, to remind me if it had not been for the angels' protection, Li'l Harry would have been hurt much more severely—and could have even been killed! At this point, I stopped asking where the angels had been and began to thank God for His protection. I thanked God for sending the angels to do their job.

You may be asking, as I was, "Why don't guardian angels 'guard' us from *all* harm? Why do angels just make it not as bad as it could have been, as opposed to stopping it from happening altogether?" I don't know the answers in full. I do know that we live in a fallen world and even righteous people are the victims of the sin of others, both in our present generation and in past generations.

I know that we can limit angel activity in several ways:

(1) We tie the hands of our angels by refusing to fulfill the vows we make before God.

*When you make a vow to God, do not delay to pay it.... Better not to vow than to vow and not pay. Do not let your mouth cause your flesh to sin, nor say before the messenger of God that it was an error...* (Ecclesiastes 5:4-6 NKJV).

(2) We limit angels when we purposefully break the laws of society or purposefully attempt to defy natural law. (We find very few instances of angels helping those who break natural or societal law as an act of their wills. By contrast, stories of angelic intervention are quite common in accidental events.)

(3) We can limit angels by our own greed or by seeking to have our own way.

*Whoever seeks to save his life will lose it, and whoever loses his life will preserve it* (Luke 17:33 NKJV).

(4) We limit angels when we fail to adhere to God's Word or to place our trust in God. So, again, I cannot answer all the whys. But we must conclude that there are limitations and stipulations regarding the protective power of angels, and most of those relate to our own *response to the Lord.*[1]

It's funny, when something goes wrong, we automatically need someone to blame. And in this incidence with Li'l Harry, I thought the angels were good candidates! I was so prone to think in terms of nothing going wrong where my children were concerned and everything being perfect for them, I had forgotten what could have happened if it had not been for the angels.

God ever so sweetly let me discover this beautiful truth when I quit needing someone to blame. Blame is really an ugly thing and is rooted and based in pride. When I didn't want to deal with it possibly being my fault, I did a very human thing and looked for another source to blame! The angels were a very easy target because they weren't my Father God, and they weren't my husband or myself.

I have since asked God to help me accept His love, protection, and correction without getting under pride, blame, or shame. I want to be free to act like the Father God and receive from the Father God everything He has for me. I want to be in a position to receive angelic protection and direction whenever the Father sends it!

Whether we know it or not, whether we believe it or not, whether we want them or not, angels are all around us doing the will of the Father where our lives are concerned. I have made it a habit to include in my daily prayers over our children, "Thank You, Father God, for sending four angels to guard, guide, direct, and protect each of our children." You might ask, why four angels? At this point in our lives I could just imagine the four directions from each of our children, north, south, east, and west. I wanted at least one angel in each direction, flanked like a wall of protection around them. Now I may ask for 10 angels, or 100, or many more. When our son Roman prays now, I hear him ask the Lord each and every time for 20 angels per person he is praying for! As I have gotten older, I am not nearly as specific as I am constant, and faithful. There is something about assigning a number when we pray though that makes it seem that much more personal and real!

I would never be so presumptuous as to assume that the angels take orders from me. They do not! They do take orders from my Father God and many times are sent because of my mouth—whether that be by prayer or confession of God's Word. My words are heard and the angels are sent on assignment (or not sent on assignment) by the God who created them.

The bottom line is we do our part by walking in obedience to the Word of God and relying on the sovereignty of God. And God's protection may not come the way we think it should. A classic illustration of that is the story of Daniel and the lions' den.

*My God sent His angel and shut the lions' mouths, so that they have not hurt me, because I was found innocent before Him; and also, O king, I have done no wrong before you* (Daniel 6:22 NKJV).

God shut the mouths of the lions so they wouldn't eat Daniel. He did this by sending an angel to do the job. The angels must have been strong! The lions were being starved so they would jump on whoever was thrown into the pit and eat them. The angels shut the huge mouths of hungry lions in order to protect Daniel.

When the pit was opened the next morning, God's divine protection was revealed. Daniel had been in there all night with those starved lions, and they had not even tried to eat him or tear him apart with their claws. They were relaxed, comfortable, and had not touched a hair on Daniel's head! God has His ways and they are definitely higher than ours!

Yes, God promises protection, but He may not do it the way you would choose. I'm sure Daniel would have preferred to have been kept out of the lions' den altogether, but that's not the way God chose to do it. We must trust God and His methods.

Sometimes His protection comes in the midst of "a lions' den." As he was thrown into the lions' den, I'm sure Daniel would have agreed with Jesus' words in Matthew 19:26: *"With men this is impossible, but with God all things are possible"* (NKJV). Sometimes it looks as though all is lost and impossibility has taken over. Daniel faced what seemed to be impossible! Yet when your situations become *impossible,* God intervenes, dissects the word, and respells *"I'm possible!"* Impossibilities become possible with God on our side. Just look at Daniel's deliverance and be encouraged.

## ENDNOTE

1. Phil Phillips, *Angels, Angels, Angels* (Starburst, 1995), 47-51.

# 12

## ANGELS EXCEL IN STRENGTH

In Philippians 4:13 we read, "We can do all things through Christ who strengthens us" (author's paraphrase). If angels are warring for us, they had better be strong, especially if they are fighting for Cheryl. Lord knows she needs the strongest of angels to protect her. Just think about what she has survived and how...especially before I learned how to spiritually protect and cover her. I now know I have a godly right and place as the head of our home to keep my wife and children supernaturally covered through the power of God!

— *Harry Salem II*

We mentioned in the last chapter the fact that the angels must have literally shut the mouths of the lions when Daniel was thrown into the lions' den. That took an excellent strength! Besides, Daniel was in the lions' den all night. Holding a lion's mouth shut for a short period of time would be an unbelievable accomplishment—much less holding it shut for an entire night!

Psalm 103:20 says, *"Bless the Lord, you His angels, who excel in strength, who do His word, heeding the voice of His word"* (NKJV). According to God's Word, angels are strong. They are not weaklings without abilities to accomplish great tasks for God. There is no man on the earth or demon in hell, including the devil himself, who can outwit or outwrestle the angelic forces of God.

The Angel that wrestled with Jacob and threw Jacob's hip out of socket was no wimpy little soprano-singing, harp-strummin', namby-pamby!

> *And Jacob was left alone, and a Man wrestled with him until daybreak. And when [the Man] saw that he did not prevail against [Jacob], He touched the hollow of his thigh; and Jacob's thigh was put out of joint as he wrestled with Him. Then He said, Let Me go, for day is breaking. But [Jacob] said, I will not let You go unless You declare a blessing upon me* (Genesis 32:24-26).

Which one of the Godhead can we touch? Which one can contend with us until our nature changes? This Angel Man was Jesus!

Jacob was wrestling with the Angel (Jesus), contending with God at his time of desperate need. Jacob knew God had willed to bless him, and he would settle for nothing less than his full inheritance. In this time of wrestling, Jacob's name, which meant "supplanter," is changed to *Israel*, meaning "he will rule as God" (Hebrew/Greek) or "contender with God" (AMP). God commends Jacob for his prevailing attitude; he is a fighter.[1] From Genesis 32:28 we read:

*And He said, Your name shall be called no more Jacob [sup-planter], but Israel [contender with God]; for you have contended and have power with God and with men and have prevailed.*

God loves a tenacious spirit, and His Word shows us how. *"... He is a rewarder of them that diligently seek Him"* (Heb. 11:6 KJV).

Jacob wrestled with God until God changed his name and ultimately changed his destiny. This Angel (Jesus) was so strong that Jacob's hip was pulled completely out of the socket!

Here's another passage that depicts the strength of angels.

*And behold, there was a great earthquake; for an angel of the Lord descended from heaven, and came and rolled back the stone from the door, and sat on it* (Matthew 28:2 NKJV).

When the angel came upon the scene, his presence caused an earthquake—and he rolled back a stone that covered the entire entrance to the tomb where Jesus was laid. He then proceeded to move the stone out of the way! Jesus didn't need the stone moved so He could get out of the tomb. The stone was rolled away, not that Jesus could escape, but that witnesses could see the evidence of an empty tomb—and maybe to emphasize the strength of the angel!

God always has a purpose, and sometimes I think God has a flair for the dramatic. Whatever the emphasis, it took a great, big, strong, and powerful angel to move the stone.

Whenever I have seen the angels, in their physiques they always look like weightlifters. As I have previously described to you, they are always very tall (at least 10 to 12 feet tall), and they are always rippling with muscles! Any part of their physique that is exposed, depending on what garments they have on, is bursting with washboard-looking muscles. Even their facial muscles are beautifully and wondrously sculpted!

There is nothing about their appearance that seems to be weak. Everything about them gives you the feeling that they can defeat anything that gets in the way of their duty to the Father God.

Several years ago, Gabrielle and I were on our way to pick up the boys from school. We were only a mile or so away from the school when I heard the still small voice of the Holy Spirit tell me to watch the car that was about to pull out of a neighborhood just in front of me.

I could see the car, the lady driving it, and the child sitting in the front passenger's seat. She was looking right at me, but just as our car was even with hers, she pulled out right toward the side of our car! She was so close to me that I saw everything in her front seat.

I never moved the steering wheel, but our vehicle was moved over horizontally so that her car did not hit us! She didn't even scratch our vehicle! She had the most surprised look on her face when she realized what she had done. Our angels definitely are strong!

There was a man just ahead of us who was working on some electrical lines. He had seen the entire incident. As I slowly pulled up alongside him, he commented on my tremendous driving skills. He said that he had never seen a car move over in that manner. Our angels pushed our car horizontally at just the right time. They did a great job!

Angels are always doing their jobs. They are consistently obedient to the Father God. Psalm 103:20 says, *"Praise the Lord, you His angels, you mighty ones who do His bidding, who obey His word"* (NIV).

You may be recalling some of the tragedies that I have written about in this book. You may be saying, "How could you say they constantly protected you? You were crippled from a car wreck. You were scarred all over your face. You were sexually abused for ten years of your childhood. You miscarried a baby. You lost your daughter at the age of 6. How can you call that protection?"

I am still standing, am I not? Obviously, at the time of those traumas in my life, I (like Daniel in the lions' den) would have preferred to not go through those difficulties and the grief. However, not only am I standing, God has restored me! According to *Webster's Dictionary, to restore* means to "bring back to a former or original condition." When something is restored in the Scriptures, however, it is always increased, multiplied, or improved so that its latter state is significantly better than its original state.

> *Fear not, O land; be glad and rejoice, for the Lord has done great things!*
>
> *Be not afraid, you wild beasts of the field, for the pastures of the wilderness have sprung up and are green; the tree bears its fruit, and the fig tree and the vine yield their [full] strength.*
>
> *Be glad then, you children of Zion, and rejoice in the Lord, your God; for He gives you the former or early rain in just measure and in righteousness, and He causes to come down for you the rain, the former rain and the latter rain, as before.*
>
> *And the [threshing] floors shall be full of grain and the vats shall overflow with juice [of the grape] and oil.*

*And I will restore or replace for you the years that the locust has eaten—the hopping locust, the stripping locust, and the crawling locust, My great army which I sent among you.*

*And you shall eat in plenty and be satisfied and praise the name of the Lord, your God, Who has dealt wondrously with you. And My people shall never be put to shame* (Joel 2:21-26).

God multiplies when He restores! Therefore, when God restores, it means it is "better than original"! I am a *restored* vessel for the Lord. That means I am better than I was before! Glory! Therefore I praise Him for the trials that I have gone through and the restoration He has done in my life.

What the devil meant for destruction, God has turned around as blessings in my life. God has truly worked all things together for my good.

*We are assured and know that [God being a partner in their labor] all things work together and are [fitting into a plan] for good to and for those who love God and are called according to [His] design and purpose* (Romans 8:28).

Any one of those disasters could have brought death to me, but they didn't. I could have been killed in the tragic car wreck, but the Lord miraculously healed me and has allowed me to share my healing testimony all over the world during my reign as Miss America 1980 and still to this day. The sexual abuse in my childhood could have destroyed my life emotionally, but now God is using my story of deliverance to minister to thousands. We lost a precious baby boy before we could even hold or cuddle him, but God let me see him in a vision standing before the Lord as a man. He also gave us a precious baby daughter, Gabrielle, within the following year.

And even though we don't fully understand (but God does!) the reason Gabrielle went home to be with Him at the age of 6 in November 1999, we know with total assurance that she's in the presence of the Lord and that she's healthy and whole now.

With God's help, we walked through that valley of grief together after her death, and He sustained us.

And I want to repeat what I said after miscarrying our son. It may appear to many that we lost our battle when Gabrielle died, and while we ourselves don't yet comprehend the reason for it, we know that we'll only be separated from her for a short time before we join her in Heaven.

Until then we can minister to the needs of many more people than ever before because of the walk of faith we took with Gabrielle the last 11 months of her life. We came out victoriously, we're filled with a deeper compassion for others than ever, and we still love and trust God with our whole hearts.

Any one of those horrible acts of the devil against me could have made me quit, give up, and lay my calling down. Yet I didn't.

Through the power of the Holy Spirit, the intervention of the angels of God, and the *blood of the Lamb,* I have remained victorious in Jesus. Thank God for the protection, direction, and guidance of His heavenly hosts.

## Endnote

1. Jack W. Hayford, exec. ed., *Spirit-Filled Life Bible* (Nashville: Thomas Nelson, 1991), Commentary, 5.

# 13

## ANGELIC PROTECTION: LI'L HARRY BELIEVES!

When Cheryl started seeing the angels in 1992, I was not in the right place spiritually to be able to see them. There were times when she would say to me, "Can you see the angels up there?" I would look and look and squint and squint up at the ceiling until someone would ask me if there was something wrong with my eyes. You see, I was trying to see in the natural realm what I could not comprehend in the spiritual realm.

Then came the morning when my son, Li'l Harry, saw an angel in our house. Being the logical, black-and-white thinker that I am, my first reaction was, "OK, he heard his momma talking about angels and now he thinks it's cool to see angels, too!" But when I heard Li'l Harry describe what he had seen in such simple, childlike terms, there was no doubt in my mind that he had in fact seen into the spiritual realm. I know my children, and it is true what the Scriptures say: And a little child shall lead them.

— *Harry Salem II*

As you know by reading this book, I needed protection! (Don't we all!) During my reign as Miss America in 1980 there were numerous death threats, assaults, and attacks against my life. I never worried about my future. I knew that God's hand was upon my life, and my destiny was not finished. God so graciously sent the angels to protect, guide, and direct me through it all. In fact, when I gave my final walk as Miss America on the runway in Atlantic City, I was surrounded by at least one dozen police officers. I thank God for the police officers, but I had "the peace that surpasses all understanding" because of my trust in the Lord and His protection.

> *And the peace of God, which surpasses all understanding, will guard your hearts and minds through Christ Jesus* (Philippians 4:7 NKJV).

You see, there was a death threat on my life even that week! A policewoman slept in the room with me, but my peace and security were not in human protection. I knew that God's angels were watching over me, and I would complete my mission on this earth. No demon in hell can stop the work of the Father God in my life as long as I am submitted and committed to my relationship with Him. No demon can stop God's work in your life, either!

Since the first time I saw my own guardian angel and he appeared with such strength, I have never been afraid. I know that the angels are watching over me, my husband, and my children. I know that we can rest at night and feel secure during the day that our protectors appointed by our heavenly Father are taking care of us and helping us to accomplish what God has called us to do for His glory.

My life seems to represent one mountain after another, and my own guardian angel, Gabion, has probably had to call upon reinforcements many times throughout the years of my warfaring life. Just as Gabriel and Michael worked together to get the message delivered to Daniel, I'm sure there is continual teamwork in the supernatural realm on our behalf.

According to my studies of the Word of God, angels have many duties and responsibilities. They are capable of performing many tasks, but they take their directions directly from the throne of God. We cannot order them around, but we can ask the Father God to send them out to do their jobs according to God's Word. It's important that we enlist the angels on behalf of our families through God's Word.

Harry and I prayed over our children every night, and we prayed for God's divine protection to be activated. We varied the words slightly each evening, but we covered the same ground each time. We prayed, "Father, we thank You, in the name of Jesus, for our precious gifts in our children. We bless them in the name of the Father, Son, and Holy Ghost. We pray Your anointing will rest upon their lives. We ask You, Father, to put Your angels around them to guard, guide, and direct them throughout the days and nights of their lives. We praise You for the call of God that rests upon them, and we ask You to stir up the gifts that are placed within them for Your service." Sometimes we would continue to quote the entire 91st Psalm over our children using their names to personalize the passage, "Li'l Harry (Roman) *dwells in the secret place of the Most High and abides in the shadow of the Almighty."*

Just as we prayed the Word of God over our children, we were teaching them to quote the Scriptures in their prayers. Even as small boys they began their individual prayers with Psalm 103:1, *"Bless the Lord, O my soul; and all that is within me, bless His holy name!"* (NKJV). This helped them to begin to practice speaking God's Word into their lives. We wanted them to know that when we ask according to His Word, He hears and answers!

> *Now this is the confidence that we have in Him, that if we ask anything according to His will, He hears us. And if we know that He hears us, whatever we ask, we know that we have the petitions that we have asked of Him* (1 John 5:14-15 NKJV).

As we claimed God's Word in Psalm 91 that He will give His angels charge over our children to keep them in all their ways, our children have grown to understand that God may use His angels to give them direction. Our sons are grown men now, and they know how to pray for themselves and for us! But they are still our sons, and we continue to pray for them, no matter how old they become.

Not long after I began to see the angels in the services, I began to notice considerable supernatural activity in our home that was not necessarily seen or even felt by everyone. Sometimes I would see the angels walk down the upstairs hallway toward the boys' room. When I would run out into the hall to get a better view, I wouldn't see them any longer. You may be saying, "Now I know for sure this Cheryl Salem has gone off the deep end!" I want you to know I was fully awake during these incidents, and they would sometimes take place in the middle of the day!

One morning I was going about my normal morning routine getting Li'l Harry ready for school, going over homework, getting breakfast prepared, fixing lunch boxes, etc., when Li'l Harry said to me, "Mommy, is Tracey up yet?" Tracey Jacobs was a daily part of our family. She moved in with us one month before our second son, Roman, was born. She helped us in every part of our lives and ministry, and especially with the children. I said that she was not and asked why he wanted to know. Then he wanted to know if Daddy was up. I told him no and that he (Li'l Harry) and I were the only ones up. He said to me, "Then that must have been an angel walking down the kitchen hallway." He was so matter of fact and so calm.

I asked him why he would think so, and could he describe to me what he had seen? He said, "Sure, Mom." He then proceeded to tell me that he had seen a person in what he described as a white robe or housecoat going out of the kitchen toward the garage. I asked him why he would think that it was an angel. He said, "Oh, I know what angels look like. They come into my room sometimes at night when I am lonely for you or scared. They tell me to not worry and to go back to sleep. They tell me that they are keeping guard over me and Roman so we can rest."

You could have knocked me over with a feather! My seven-year-old child was talking to the angels in our home and was at total ease with them! I sat down and told him much of what I had been experiencing with the angels, and he was not at all shocked. Why can't we adults accept God's provisions like children do? We come on the earth with the ability to use great faith. As we grow we are supposed to mature, but what many believers have done is learn how to doubt! Oh, if only we, as Christian adults, would receive the truth about the supernatural like the children, then we could take the truth to the people of the world.

# 14

## ANGELS WATCHING OVER GABRIELLE

Cheryl was so sick that she was bedfast after delivering Gabrielle and then battling with Gabrielle's sleep apnea. If ever there was a time whenIneededtoknowangelswereinourhome,it wasduringthistime.Istillhaven'tseenthem,butI knowthatIknowtheyaretherewatchingoverour family day and night—and not from a distance!

— *Harry Salem II*

Visitations from the angels had become almost commonplace in our home. Not that we took it lightly or for granted, but we became accustomed to it. They were not seen every day, but as I said in the last chapter, many times one of us saw them walking down the hallway or around a corner.

These visits helped me to understand and to teach others the importance of *not* worshiping the angels. They are not to be worshiped. They are ministering servants like Hebrews 1:14 says, but they are *not* in any way, shape, or form gods! God and God alone is to be worshiped, praised, and adored. He is the only true God!

The angels cannot be summoned, called upon, or ordered around by us on this earth. They take their orders directly from the throne room of our God and Father. I have said this time and time again, but it is important that it sink deep into our hearts.

God has given the angels as a protective benefit for us, and I want to activate that benefit to the fullest. God's divine protection is such a source of comfort to me especially when our children were small, because, as a mother, it was sometimes difficult to minister, travel, and preach the good news when it required leaving our children at home. So, I was and still am very thankful for the angels and my husband.

Harry is such a wonderful father and husband. I am so grateful for the active role he takes in all of our lives. Yet, as he and I have matured in the Lord, we are both called to service more and more. This required truly trusting in God's protection of our children when we had to temporarily leave them in someone else's care when they were small. As parents, the only rest and assurance we have is knowing God's Word is working in all of our lives and that it will not return null or void!

> So shall My word be that goes forth from My mouth; it shall not return to Me void, but it shall accomplish what I please, and it shall prosper in the thing for which I sent it (Isaiah 55:11 NKJV).

As I said in the last chapter, Li'l Harry had seen the angels on numerous occasions. But the rest of the family just knew by faith that they were with us. Faith is enough to relax and enjoy God! On one occasion I was out of town ministering. Tracey Jacobs, who lived with us and is like our very own daughter, was with Gabrielle during her nighttime-learning-how-to-sleep lesson. (A good sleeping pattern has never come with birth for our children.) We had been working with Gabrielle for several nights by this time, and she was finally developing a better sleep pattern. It was taking incredible diligence and consistency. At times, we weren't sure if we were making any progress. However, by faith we knew that if we stuck with it, the crying would eventually stop, and she would understand what we were trying to do.

For some reason, on this particular night she was crying out, apparently in her sleep, just a little at a time. After several outbursts, Tracey decided she should go to her room and check to make sure her needs were met. She stood outside the door, instead of entering the room, and listened for any signs of distress.

It was the middle of the night and all the lights were off in the house. Gabrielle's room had a blackout curtain on the window so when the sun came up in the mornings, the sunlight wouldn't awaken her. There was no way for light to enter her room from the outside.

Just as Tracey was about to go back to her own room, a very bright light flashed under Gabrielle's door! At first Tracey tried to rationalize what the light could have been, but there was no "normal" explanation for the occurrence.

She thought maybe a car had been on the road and the headlights had illuminated the room. That was impossible because of the angle of Gabrielle's window to the road. Plus, the blackout curtain, mini-blinds, and regular curtain that hung on her window would have never allowed any penetration from an outside source of light.

As Tracey stood there thinking, the Holy Spirit spoke to her and said for her not to be afraid. He told her she had seen the brilliance of the angels who were watching over Gabrielle. Immediately an indescribable peace settled over Tracey. She told me from that moment on she knew she didn't have to worry. The angels were watching over all of the children, and God was in control of our household.

Tracey opened the door anyway and went into Gabrielle's room. She checked every possible solution to the origin of the bright white light, but there was no explanation except the brilliance of the angels' presence.

This experience was such a source of reassurance for Harry and me, and for Tracey, who kept our children when we had to be away. The Father God opened Tracey's eyes in the spirit to reassure us all that His angels were protecting the children. The angels really do watch over us all!

# 15

# WHY DO ANGELS LOOK LIKE THEY DO?

Remember that the first thing God said was, "Let there be light," and there was. Light and color are God's way of showing us just how great He is. If He could create the beauty of this earth, then the brilliance of the angels from Heaven must be a billion times brighter and more colorful and majestic. If man on this earth is a rainbow of different skin colors, why not the angelic realm as well? Don't discount God's masterful creative abilities, or satan's counterfeit nature. God is light and satan is darkness.

— *Harry Salem II*

I have seen the angels many times since 1992. I tried to the best of my limited vocabulary to portray their indescribably magnificent beauty and splendor in Chapter I—where I described the angels I saw in Buffalo, New York. The Bible also describes their appearance, so let's take a look.

Just as I saw the angels enter with bursts of light into the sanctuary in Buffalo, the apostle John describes an angel coming forth with bright light. Revelation 18:1 declares, *"Then I saw another angel descending from heaven, possessing great authority, and the earth was illuminated with his radiance and splendor."*

Angels exude light. It seems to come from the core of their being. It's like they glow from the inside out! However, the illumination that comes from within them does not white out their appearance. You can still see their outline, the details of their features and the garments they are wearing.

When Li'l Harry saw the angels in our home, he described them basically the same way each time. They always looked like they were filled with light. Matthew 28:3 says, *"His countenance was like lightning, and his clothing as white as snow"* (NKJV).

The best way I know to describe their "lightning" appearance is by comparing it to looking into a spotlight. When looking into a spotlight, you can somewhat make out the features around the light, but you can also see the brilliance of the light. The big difference is that the angels are not earthly matter. They are not dimensional by human standards. *"And of the angels He says: 'Who makes His angels spirits and His ministers a flame of fire?'"* (Heb. 1:7 NKJV).

The *World Book Encyclopedia* states that "light is a form of energy (the ability to do work) that can travel freely through space."[1] That sounds like the angels! That is why, even though the angels are not made of substance or matter, they can move rocks!

When you look at angelic beings, they are giving off light, but it does not consume their features. You are looking right at them, and yet you are looking right through them all at the same time.

Of course, every analogy can break down, but I thought of one that may help you understand the angelic realm. When we fly into the Los Angeles area, I look out the window of the plane when we are within range of landing. At that viewpoint, I can actually see the smog that covers that city like a blanket. It is very easy to see! Yet when I am on the ground, I don't see the smog at all (unless I look into the distance). It's there, but for the most part, I just can't see it.

The angelic realm is very much like this. It is all around us—like a parallel realm so to speak. Most of the time no one can see the angelic realm. Generally, it will never be seen by the majority of people no matter how spiritual or "in tune" they seem to be. But that does not change the existence of it any more than saying that air does not exist because you can't see it (unless you live in the Los Angeles area!).

The angelic realm is real. It does exist for our benefit, and I plan to utilize everything God has made available for me. In further searching the *World Book Encyclopedia* on the subject of light and color, I found these remarks quite interesting.

Phosphorescence is a process by which "atoms absorb light energy from one source and then give off their own light."[2]  In simple terms, phosphorescence is a process in which energy absorbed by a substance is released relatively slowly in the form of light. This is in some cases the mechanism used for "glow-in-the-dark" materials that are "charged" by exposure to light. Unlike the relatively swift reactions in a common fluorescent tube, phosphorescent materials used for these materials absorb the energy and "store" it for a longer time as the processes required to re-emit the light occur less often.[3] That sounds like what God does through the angels, doesn't it? The angels absorb light energy from God and reflect it.

The other statement I found intriguing years ago when I first started studying this was, "All colors in the spectrum mixed together form white light."[4] Isaac Newton proved this when he took a prism and separated each color of the spectrum by using a beam of white light. White is the culmination of all colors mixed together.

Remember when I described the angels that I saw in Buffalo? They were illuminating bright multicolored lights! I couldn't quite make this fit with the other Scriptures that talked about light but never mentioned colored lights, until I found the Scripture in Revelation 10:1 that refers to the angels:

> And I saw another mighty angel come down from heaven, clothed with a cloud: and a rainbow was upon his head, and his face was as it were the sun, and his feet as pillars of fire (KJV).

These were the angels I saw in Buffalo! They were multicolored like the rainbow. And yet there was a burst of bright, white light when they entered or left the building. This was an example of Newton's proving that white is the culmination of all colors mixed together.

As I have seen both angels and demons, I have often wondered why the angels give off light and the demons are filled with the blackest darkness. As I meditated on God's Word, the Holy Spirit led me to a Scripture that I think reveals some insight to this question.

*Take heed that ye despise not one of these little ones; for I say unto you, That in heaven their angels do always behold the face of My Father which is in heaven* (Matthew 18:10 KJV).

I began to think about these little ones' angels that are ever in the face of the Father.

Then I thought about Luke 1:19 where the Scripture says:

*...I am Gabriel. I stand in the [very] presence of God, and I have been sent to talk to you and to bring you this good news.*

Yes, the angels come and go, but they spend the majority of their time "beholding the face of the Father which is in heaven."

As I read these Scriptures over and over, it was made so clear to me. Angels live in the presence of God! The angels get their illuminated appearance from being in the presence of the Father God. All the angels are full of the illumination of God. This also explains the feelings of peace, contentment and relaxation that exude from their very being.

I believe the demons (fallen angels) are full of darkness because they have been completely cut off from the presence of the Father, making them lose all of their once-present illumination. That's why angels always put off light and demons have no light at all. And I believe that is why the demons are generally small in size, hideous in appearance, gnarled, scarred, and slimy.

How the demons must hate the angels, knowing that at one time their countenances were also filled with the glory of God. Because of the demons' (fallen angels) inability to be near the Father God, they have no light, no life, no beauty. Only death, destruction, ugliness, sickness, and disease fill their beings. What a horrible hell of an existence for all of eternity!

When I first began my research on all of this, my main source of information was of course, the Bible, followed by the *World Book Encyclopedia 1973 edition.* Now I have the Internet and a vast amount of information at my finger tips. But that does not discount what I learned many years ago. *The World Book* gave several definitions for words that seemed to describe angelic and demonic interaction with God's light or lack of it. *Transparent* means "light can pass through it." *Translucent* means "an object that scatters the light that is passed through it" (like frosted glass). *Opaque* means "an object that does not permit light to pass through it."[5] Think with me about the words *translucent* and *opaque* and how satan may try to deceive you. The word *translucent* could be satan's deceptive interaction with God's real light, causing a counterfeit. The word *opaque* could be satan's interacting with God's light by a total blinding to the truth.

I have often wondered about the Scripture that says to beware of satan masquerading as an angel of light. *"And it is no wonder, for Satan himself masquerades as an angel of light"* (2 Cor. 11:14).

How could this be possible? My answer came from God's Word. When studying, meditating, and reading, we need to learn to pay close attention to detail and to pray for the revelation of God to awaken our minds to the true meanings for us.

But let's take a look at several different Scriptures that are remarkable to me.

> Now there was a day when the sons of God came to present themselves before the Lord, and Satan came also among them. And the Lord said unto Satan, Whence comest thou? Then Satan answered the Lord, and said, From going to and fro in the earth, and from walking up and down in it (Job 1:6-7 KJV).

*Again there was a day when the sons of God [the angels] came to present themselves before the Lord, and Satan (the adversary and the accuser) came also among them to present himself before the Lord* (Job 2:1).

*...For the accuser of our brethren, he who keeps bringing before our God charges against them day and night, has been cast out!* (Revelation 12:10)

Just by looking at these three Scriptures it seems to me that only satan has access to God's throne and not all of his demons and devils. He stands before the throne and brings charges against you and me before the Father God. But remember, this access is only temporary, as seen in the following additional Scriptures:

*And there was war in heaven: Michael and his angels fought against the dragon; and the dragon fought and his angels,*

*And prevailed not; neither was their place found any more in heaven.*

*And the great dragon was cast out, that old serpent, called the Devil, and Satan, which deceiveth the whole world: he was cast out into the earth, and his angels were cast out with him.*

*And I heard a loud voice saying in heaven, Now is come salvation, and strength, and the kingdom of our God, and the power of His Christ: for the accuser of our brethren is cast down, which accused them before our God day and night.*

*And they overcame him by the blood of the Lamb, and by the word of their testimony; and they loved not their lives unto the death.*

*Therefore rejoice, ye heavens, and ye that dwell in them. Woe to the inhabiters of the earth and of the sea! for the devil is come down unto you, having great wrath, because he knoweth that he hath but a short time* (Revelation 12:7-12 KJV).

*And the devil that deceived them was cast into the lake of fire and brimstone, where the beast and the false prophet are, and shall be tormented day and night for ever and ever* (Revelation 20:10 KJV).

This makes me so grateful that Jesus stands at the right hand of God ever making intercession for us who have trusted Christ for our salvation.

*Who is he that condemneth? It is Christ that died, yea rather, that is risen again, who is even at the right hand of God, who also maketh intercession for us* (Romans 8:34 KJV).

*Wherefore He is able also to save them to the uttermost that come unto God by Him, seeing He ever liveth to make intercession for them* (Hebrews 7:25 KJV).

For every accusation that satan can come up with, Jesus is our "defense attorney" and He pleads our case to the Father God. Because of the blood of the Lamb, we are forevermore forgiven and cleansed from all unrighteousness. We can stand before God knowing that we are covered in the blood of Jesus; and when we are presented before the Father, all He sees is Jesus' blood. Now that's something to shout about!

Because of the devil's (satan himself) ability to go before the Father God, it is a possibility that satan receives some portion of God's illumination on him, thus giving him the ability to pretend to be an "angel of light," when all he wants is to bring confusion, destruction, or desolation. We do know for certain that satan does *deceive* under the pretense of being one of God's angelic messengers. The word to notice is *masquerade* or pretend. Satan is not an angel of light. He can only *pretend* to be an angel of light.

The Word is full of treasures that give us different details about why angels look the way they do. Hopefully, I have ignited your interest to further dig in His Word about the subject. I know for sure that God keeps the treasures in His Word for us—not from us. It's just up to us to commit ourselves to daily "dig in His garden," to help us master the Word, and then to be mastered by it!

## ENDNOTES

1. *World Book Encyclopedia* (Field Enterprises Educ. Corp.,1973); Vol. 12-L, 249.

2. Ibid., 249.

3. http://en.wikipedia.org/wiki/Phosphorescence.

4. *World Book Encyclopedia;* Vol. 12-L, 249.

5. Ibid., 250b.

# 16

# Things That Go "Bump" in the Night

Angels in my bedroom and she didn't wake me up! Now she's getting messages for other people—nothing for me. I'm still waiting to see an angel, and so should you!

— *Harry Salem II*

Shortly after Tracey had seen the brilliance of the angels' presence coming from Gabrielle's room, I began to see the angels in our home more and more. They began to come into our bedroom at night and wake me up to talk to me. My sweetheart who sleeps very lightly never heard a sound. He never moved a muscle. Harry would even say to me later, "Why didn't you wake me?" Each time I told him that they didn't tell me to wake him, so I didn't!

On one specific occasion, they gave me a message for someone else. They came in, awakened me, and told me I was to give this message to another person in ministry. I couldn't help but think, *Why don't you go and tell him? Why are you telling me to tell him?* They didn't respond to my thoughts, and I didn't question them any further.

I really felt awkward about the entire situation. I have never been presumptuous in anything. I have always waited and listened for a confirmation before moving ahead—especially where the spirit realm is concerned. I really found myself in a dilemma.

Should I be so bold with this other person and go tell him the angels are talking to *me* about *him?* Do I say nothing and risk missing an opportunity to be obedient to the Father God? I wasn't sure what to do. When in doubt about what to do, I wait and see what God does.

After several days of deliberation, I finally decided to take the chance of offending this other person and be obedient. I always want to be sensitive to others and not just run up with a "word from the Lord" every time the wind blows. (There are people like that!)

This time I decided it is better to miss God on the side of doing *something,* rather than miss Him on the side of doing *nothing!* I questioned my motives, my heart, and the message. I knew that I was gaining nothing from delivering the message, so my motive was pure. I knew my heart was clean before the Father God. And I knew the message was nothing but a positive, affirming word from the Lord that would bring encouragement and not discouragement. After going through the steps of assurance, I knew this message was from the Lord and I was to deliver it.

Just as I had come to the decision to take action, the friend called our home very early one morning. He was already up and at the airport, about to leave on a trip to minister. Neither Harry nor I were even awake yet.

He said God had been speaking to him and had told him that the angels would be talking to me, and they would give me a message for him! Isn't God funny?

When he told this to me I began to laugh. I shared with him that an angel had already given me a message for him, and I had been debating whether to give it to him or not. He said to tell him immediately! I began to reveal to him what the angel had told me, and it was a confirmation of something the Holy Spirit had already been telling him.

First Samuel 15:22 says, *"Has the Lord as great delight in burnt offerings and sacrifices, as in obeying the voice of the Lord? Behold, to obey is better than sacrifice..."* (NKJV). I heard a Sunday school teacher say one time about this verse: "If there had been *obedience* in the Garden in the first place, there would never have been any need for a *sacrifice*." Adam and Eve disobeyed God and ate from the tree of the knowledge of good and evil. Then Jesus died to provide forgiveness and justification. This helped me understand that "obedience is better than sacrifice."

> *And to Adam He said, Because you have listened and given heed to the voice of your wife and have eaten of the tree of which I commanded you, saying, You shall not eat of it, the ground is under a curse because of you: in sorrow and toil shall you eat [of the fruits] of it all the days of your life* (Genesis 3:17).

> *For if because of one man's trespass (lapse, offense) death reigned through that one, much more surely will those who receive [God's]*

*overflowing grace (unmerited favor) and the free gift of righ-*
*teousness [putting them into right standing with Himself] reign*
*as kings in life through the one Man Jesus Christ (the Messiah,*
*the Anointed One)* (Romans 5:17).

This was the beginning of my learning to listen to the Father
God. However, He chooses to talk to me and to be obedient immediately, if necessary, to accomplish my part of God's mission upon
the earth. This was a valuable lesson as I continued to see and hear
from the angels.

My heart's desire is to respond to the voice of God with a
humble and submissive faith—like Mary did when she was vis-
ited by the angel Gabriel. When Gabriel told her that she would
conceive and would give birth to the Savior of the world, she only
responded in faith. Mary's only question was simply a "how" question, *"Then Mary said to the angel, 'How can this be, since I do not know*
*a man?'"* (Luke 1:34 NKJV).

When the angel answered her one question, Mary responded
in a pure, humble faith, *"Behold the maidservant of the Lord! Let it be to*
*me according to your word"* (Luke 1:38 NKJV). Wow! It makes my
eyes well up with tears to picture that scene. Oh, how I want that
kind of humble and pure heart toward the Father God!

# 17

# ANGELS PRAISE GOD, TOO!

No one has any idea what a responsibility it is to be trusted by God to see into the spiritual realm and to receive messages from God through the angels. I am so proud of Cheryl and the obedience in which she has walked these past years. Believe me it has not been easy for her or for our family. There have been times when the cost almost seemed more than we could bear, but I can truly say it has been worth it all.

Angels are here to help us, not to be worshiped and praised. If we will praise and worship the Father, then maybe we will see angels, too! Psalm 100:4 says, "Enter into His gates with thanksgiving, and into His courts with praise…" (NKJV).

— *Harry Salem* II

In the fall of 1992 we were in California for a worship service. Everything was proceeding as scheduled, and the services were wonderful. I arrived on the second day because of another ministry opportunity I had participated in the previous evening in Virginia Beach, Virginia. Pregnant now with Gabrielle, only a few months after Malachi had gone on to be with Jesus, I was tired, and extremely sick with flu and laryngitis. The trip was hard and exhausting for a normal person, much less someone pregnant!

I just wanted to lie down and sleep and rest. The problem was I have never known how to say that I'm tired and need a rest. I have never known how to rest when I have the opportunity. I used to push and push my body until it collapsed! This time was no different than any other.

The Saturday evening services began without a problem. Then I stood up to do my part and couldn't sing at all! Thank God for the anointing regardless of our situations and circumstances. I sat back down, feeling totally defeated and useless. I was beating myself up on the inside with self-judgment and condemnation. I convinced myself that I was of no use to anyone, including the ministry and my Father God.

And yet in spite of the big ol' pity-party that I was throwing for myself (I was the only guest at this pity-party, and no one else wanted to come!), here came the angels by the hundreds. Can you believe it? Right in the middle of my "poor me" party, the angels showed up and filled the entire ceiling area of the building! There they were with the glory of God beaming from their presence!

The church we were ministering in was built in a round shape, and the angels circled the entire auditorium several hundred deep. They stood at attention with weapons, in their ever-present military fashion that I was becoming accustomed to seeing. They flanked shoulder to shoulder, arm to arm, as if ready for action.

The singers were leading in praise and worship—and as the anointing came upon me, my voice became stronger and stronger. There is nothing sweeter than praising and worshiping God. As the people began to enter into praise to the Father God, the most amazing thing began to take place. The angels who were standing in a "secret service" stance began lifting their hands, worshiping, and singing the most beautiful song of praise to the Father God that I have ever heard! They were actually praising the Father with hands lifted, singing in an angelic language, and clapping in pure adoration! *"Though I speak with the tongues of men and of angels..."* (1 Cor. 13:1 NKJV).

No matter how sick I was, I couldn't help but rejoice with the heavenly host proclaiming Jesus as Lord of all! Immediately the Scripture in Psalm 148:2, *"Praise ye Him, all His angels: praise ye Him, all His hosts"* (KJV), exploded within my spirit. I was seeing the angels praise and worship the King of kings!

Later, as I studied Scriptures concerning what I had seen, I remembered the Scripture dealing with the birth of our Lord and Savior, Jesus Christ. After seeing the angels worship, I had no trouble envisioning that wondrous scene so long ago.

> *Then suddenly there appeared with the angel an army of the troops of heaven (a heavenly knighthood), praising God and saying, Glory to God in the highest [heaven], and on earth peace among men with whom He is well pleased [men of goodwill, of His favor]* (Luke 2:13-14).

Another Scripture that depicts the angels in worship is Revelation 7:11: *"And all the angels stood round about the throne, and about the elders and the four beasts, and fell before the throne on their faces, and worshipped God"* (KJV).

The angels have been, are, and always will be worshiping God just as they did in Isaiah 6:3: *"And one cried unto another, and said, Holy, holy, holy, is the Lord of hosts: the whole earth is full of His glory"* (KJV).

I think it is plain to see that one of the primary functions of angels is to worship and praise the Father God. It is exciting to begin to understand some of the responsibilities of the angels. God's Word gives us so much insight into the angelic realm.

Occasionally, I see the angels in services where I am not ministering. Sometimes in our home church I will see the angels. Many times I have seen the angels and the demons at battle in ministry services throughout the country where Harry and I were ministering. Sometimes I will be in our hotel room, praying and interceding for a particular service that is about to begin, and my eyes will be opened to the spirit realm.

Most of the time, what I see in the spirit is encouraging, but sometimes it alarms me. For example, one time I was looking out our hotel room window over a Midwestern town where a famous American writer was born. He was an atheist and denounced God. He was idolized in this town and was their "claim to fame," so to speak. As I was praying and interceding before the meeting, the Father God allowed me to see into the spirit realm and see the demonic hold the demons had over this entire city. However, there was a small group of praying and believing people who had fought against hell itself to gain a small foothold in the heavenlies there.

The Lord showed me how they had been assaulted over and over because of their place in the family of God. In the spirit I could see demonic forces that had harassed, threatened, and beaten them up. Yet these people had remained faithful to the call of the Father God on their lives to that place. He had not forsaken them, nor had He given up. But He showed me that He would not make the faithful few stay there much longer. If the people did not listen to the voice of God through His servants, He would release His servants from their assignment and send them on their way. As they left, God would allow them to literally shake off the dust of their feet, and in so doing, God would be shaking off the dust of His own feet for that town and turning His back on them. *"And whosoever shall not receive you, nor hear your words, when ye depart out of that house or city, shake off the dust of your feet"* (Matt. 10:14 KJV).

I didn't share this with the people there. The Holy Spirit told me to keep it to myself. So that's what I did. Yet I saw it, and I know God showed it to me for a reason. That reason is not clear even now, but when it is important for me to remember, God will bring it back to me and tell me what to do with it then. That is called obedience. We may not understand, but we still obey. That is why seeing in the spirit realm is not easy.

There is tremendous responsibility in seeing into the supernatural realm. I suppose that is why not everyone can do it. Many are not willing to be obedient or are not mature enough to do what the Father wants them to do and say. We must learn to walk so closely in tune with the Holy Spirit that we hear His direction in every situation. We must develop keen discernment that will keep us from being deceived by the enemy. That's why there are many who are called but few are chosen—because of the cost of obedience. It's all really very simple but not easy.

# 18

## BASKING IN THE PRAISES

Cheryl and I have a personal relationship with Jesus. And when I say "personal," I mean "person-al." It's like when we were taught in school the difference between the words personal and personnel: In "personal," using the "a" meant your "pal," and in "personnel," using the "e" meant "everything else." Maybe you weren't taught that, but I was, and it's a great way to show you how Jesus is Cheryl's "Pal," because of her personal relationship with Him.

When you have a "pal type" relationship with someone, you recognize her (or his) face in a crowd, her name in conversation, even her voice on the phone. If you're as close to someone as Cheryl and I are to each other, you can recognize her by her fragrance when she has been in a room. I know Cheryl that well. So why shouldn't we be able to know Jesus that well? Be encouraged, don't be skeptical, keep your expectation high, and maybe Jesus will reveal Himself to you in a way you have never seen Him before.

— *Harry Salem II*

I moved from Nashville to Tulsa in 1985, when I married my precious husband, Harry. God had given me direction to begin ministering specifically to women on different issues, and I had seen God set thousands of women free. I had the opportunity to speak and minister to thousands of women who needed to know that God loves them just like they are. There is a way out of the mess they feel they are in, and there is healing for every hurt—including those hurts others can't see.

For several years I saw the angels at many women's conferences, though not in the numbers or magnitude as I began seeing them in 1992. And as I mentioned in an earlier chapter, twice I saw Gabion (my own guardian angel) at these meetings.

Yet one of the most profound moments in my life was when the Father God allowed me to see His Son, Jesus. I was ministering in praise and worship when I looked up and literally saw Jesus coming down the middle aisle! He was surrounded by a host of gorgeous angels. They were singing in harmonious angelic languages and gazing at Him in pure adoration. The angels were praising and worshiping Jesus just as we women were!

Jesus was absolutely basking in the praises of the women and the angels. The love that poured out to the women from our precious Savior, Jesus, was almost more than I could look upon.

How do I describe a moment like that with mere words? All I know is I have never seen such compassionate love in anyone's eyes. Jesus' eyes seemed to capture and embrace every hurt of the precious women. With each look and move of His hand, more and more peace, contentment, and healing covered the entire crowd. He moved down the aisle with a royal gentleness—a graceful strength. It was one of the most awe-inspiring and beautiful moments of my life!

As I saw Jesus start down the aisle in the back, instantly a flood of peace engulfed me. I never questioned for one second, *Who is this?* I never thought, *Is this an angel?* No. Immediately as I saw Him, I knew He was my precious Beloved, the Lover of my soul. I recognized Jesus at once and felt the warmth, love, compassion, healing, and peace that only my Savior can bring.

I can't really give you any more details, because at that moment the details seemed so unimportant. As I think back on it, all I can truly recall is the overwhelming, all-consuming feeling that permeated my very being, and I knew that all was well with my soul. Now I'll forever understand that He truly does inhabit the praises of His people—the praises of His women on that particular occasion. Psalm 22:3 says, *"But You are holy, O You Who dwell in [the holy place where] the praises of Israel [are offered]."*

# 19

# The Death Angel; For Whom Does He Work?

Here is a chapter that is really going to stretch your ability to grasp the supernatural and still believe Cheryl isn't crazy. You may be thinking, What was Harry's first reaction to this? No, it wasn't, "Cheryl, have you lost your mind?" It was, "Why didn't you wake me? Why is all this happening and I'm not involved?" It wasn't, "She's crazy." It was, "I know and believe without a shadow of a doubt, and when will I have these things revealed to me?" I couldn't wait to experience these things. I'm still waiting and still expecting....

— *Harry Salem II*

In Chapter 4, I told you about the loss of our son, Malachi, in a miscarriage. It was difficult for Harry and me to lose our baby on this earth. It was difficult to know we would have to wait until we get to Heaven to know and be with Malachi. Yet we took solace in the fact that Malachi is in the arms of Jesus. And we survived this tragedy and overcame the torment of grief by pulling together and praying.

I began to heal in my body, and we began to heal in our spirits. Sleep seemed to be the only thing that would come naturally to me, but it wouldn't stay. I was up and down all night.

About a week after the miscarriage, I was sleeping unusually soundly when I was suddenly awakened by a presence in our bedroom. I was lying still, but I knew something or someone was in our room! Since the angels had come before and awakened me, my first thought was that the angels had come for a visit. I did not feel afraid, but there was no peace in the air. Before, when the angels had come, there was immeasurable peace that permeated the air, the room, my very being.

I sat up on the side of the bed and began to focus my eyes to the dark. Then it hit me! I realized there was no presence of light in the room. The angels always gave off a very peaceful yet bright light. If it was the angels, then where was the light?

I didn't move. I just sat very still and listened. I could feel the presence of someone standing by our door leading out into the hallway. I slowly turned my head in that direction and then I saw it! There in the midst of the dark was the darkest, blackest figure I had ever seen. It was so dark that it made the darkness surrounding it seem like light!

This figure of darkness had on a long, black robe that reached to the floor and a hood over its head. My mind began to race. I told myself that I was still asleep and this was just a dream. So I sat up good and straight, shook myself fully awake, and swung my feet onto the floor.

I looked again. The figure was still there! I silently cried out to the Father to tell me who or what this was. I was not really afraid, but I was uneasy and unsettled with this thing in our bedroom. The Holy Spirit spoke up in my heart and said that this was not from God.

I thought, *Could this be the spirit of death? Whatever could it want in my house?* My mind raced through page after page in the Bible like I was scanning the pages on a computer. I was looking in my memory for references to any types of spirits that could be referred to as "death." I knew through my study that destroying angels or evil angels (like the one who killed Herod in Acts and slew 10,000 Israelites) are God's angels sent on assignment for blatant disobedience. But this dark angel was definitely not from God. There was no light, no peace—*who or what was this?* I wasn't sure, but I did know that the source of it was from the pit of hell.

I knew this black figure was trying to convince me of something. I stood up and took a few steps toward the bathroom, never taking my eyes off the ominous, body-shaped thing. My sleepy, exhausted mind was whirling 90 miles an hour! I was thinking that I wanted a better look at this thing so I continued to the bathroom and flipped on the light.

I never took my eyes off "it." I flipped on the light and "it" didn't move. Even with the bright bathroom light reflecting onto it, there was still something ominous and eerie about it. There was no fear, but I was very uncomfortable.

As I stared at the figure, which was approximately 5 feet tall, blackness all around it, hood drawn up over what would have been a head, I realized there was no face! At least, there was no face that I could see. It was only hollow and dark under the hood.

My mind was in continual turmoil. *Who is this? Why is it here? What is it? What could it want? What does this mean?* Suddenly, all of my questions were answered. I had a total and clear understanding of who and what it was. I knew what it wanted and why. I had full realization of the meaning of this presence in our home.

This was the demonic spirit who had taken our baby from us only days before when I had miscarried Malachi. I had no idea what it thought it was here for this time, but I was not going to get into conversation with it. I knew that I was to take action and take it now! Its mission was death, and it was trying to convince and deceive me just by its presence that it was here to take yet another Salem child. But I would not be deceived.

I spoke to it in the name of Jesus and commanded it to leave my house and never return. I told it that there wasn't anything in this home for it to take. *Now, get out in Jesus' name!* I silently screamed. And then I said it out loud, "Get out of this house and never return again! There is nothing for you here, in Jesus' name!" With the name of Jesus spoken, it *immediately* turned around and walked right through the wall and out of our house!

I had been in deep study and thought on the subject of angels for over a month by this time. I knew because of the absence of light that this was not sent by our Father God. I knew that because of Jesus' death and resurrection the devil once had the power of death but Jesus took back those keys. Death no longer has the victory—even in the instance of Malachi, death did not win because he is with Jesus forever. Even with our daughter, Gabrielle, she is alive forevermore.

*And the Ever-living One [I am living in the eternity of the eternities]. I died, but see, I am alive forevermore; and I possess the keys of death and Hades (the realm of the dead)* (Revelation 1:18).

You may find it interesting that no matter how hard I stared into the place under the hood where its face should have been, I couldn't see a face at all. I couldn't see anything! There was only blackness. It was shorter than me, and it made no moves to try and overpower me. In fact, it made no moves at all. The only movement the entire time was when I commanded it to go in the name of Jesus. Then it turned and departed out of our home, never to return again as far as I was concerned!

When we understand our authority through the blood of Jesus, we will walk on this earth afraid of no one or no thing. Stand your ground and begin to win against the enemy!

I'm not sure whether this "demonic angel" was really sent to kill someone or whether it was sent to make me fearful. I do know that satan preys upon people when they are their weakest and most tired.

*So for the sake of Christ, I am well pleased and take pleasure in infirmities, insults, hardships, persecutions, perplexities and distresses; for when I am weak [in human strength], then am I [truly] strong (able, powerful, in divine strength)* (2 Corinthians 12:10).

I know that *"the devil walks about like a roaring lion, seeking whom he may devour"* (I Pet. 5:8 NKJV). That's when we must rely upon the strength of the Lord to do our fighting for us and never give the enemy entry into our lives.

When this was all over, I went back to bed and slept peacefully. The next morning I told Harry what had transpired in the night, and his first reaction was, "Why didn't you wake me up?" You know, you would think that would have been my first reaction—but it never crossed my mind. All I could think about was getting that thing out of our house! Had I been afraid, I'm sure Harry would have been immediately awakened. However, at that moment I didn't feel alone. I knew that the Father God, Jesus, and the Holy Spirit were with me and had not forsaken me. I had perfect peace because I knew Jesus was with me. Isaiah 26:3 says it all for me: *"Thou wilt keep him in perfect peace, whose mind is stayed on Thee: because he trusteth in Thee"* (KJV).

Yes, and amen.

# 20

## MEN AND ANGELS' RELATIONSHIP

Here Cheryl provides some good, sound biblical teaching on the relationship we have with angels. Read this as if it is a teaching text and you will grasp more about why some people see angels.

— *Harry Salem II*

The story I shared with you in the last chapter is pretty different, but it wasn't a "scary" experience. Christians have made the supernatural realm (angels and demons) too spooky! I mentioned previously that we have been afraid to study and learn about the supernatural realm because we have been afraid of what we may find. We have to remember that God has given us the means to take authority over the devil and his demons.

Remember the Scripture in Hosea 4:6, *"My people are destroyed for lack of knowledge..."* (KJV). It's obvious that God desires for us to have knowledge so that we can make better decisions and use better judgment and discernment in our everyday lives. Something often missed in reading this Scripture is the phrase "My people." *God's own people* perish or are destroyed because they do not gain (or they reject) the knowledge that is necessary for survival.

Knowing about the supernatural realm is vital in these last days. I don't want to be deceived by anyone or anything pretending to be from God. Desperate people do desperate things. And many times their judgment is clouded by their despair and desperation.

In the next few years I believe there will be an even greater division between God's true believers and those who are not. The Bible says that there are even those who will call Him "Lord, Lord" whom He won't know. It tells us of accounts of people doing great and mighty works in His name whom He does not recognize as His sons or daughters.

> *Not everyone who says to Me, Lord, Lord, will enter the kingdom of heaven, but he who does the will of My Father Who is in heaven. Many will say to Me on that day, Lord, Lord, have we not prophesied in Your name and driven out demons in Your name and done many mighty works in Your name? And then I will say to them openly (publicly), I never knew you; depart from Me, you who act wickedly [disregarding My commands]* (Matthew 7:21-23).

> *When once the Master of the house gets up and closes the door, and you begin to stand outside and to knock at the door [again and again], saying, Lord, open to us! He will answer you, I do not know where [what household—certainly not Mine] you come from* (Luke 13:25).

*Why do you call Me, Lord, Lord, and do not [practice] what I tell you?* (Luke 6:46)

The Bible tells us of the "sheep and the goats" being separated. I want to be a sheep, not a goat! I do not want to be deceived. I want all the knowledge God has provided for me. We need to get a clear understanding of God's Word and make sure we are not in the number of God's people who perish or are destroyed because of lack of knowledge.

> *All nations will be gathered before Him, and He will separate them [the people] from one another as a shepherd separates his sheep from the goats; and He will cause the sheep to stand at His right, but the goats at His left. Then the King will say to those at His right hand, Come, you blessed of My Father [you favored of God and appointed to eternal salvation], inherit (receive as your own) the kingdom prepared for you from the foundation of the world* (Matthew 25:32-34).

After I began seeing angels, I had a hunger beyond description for scriptural knowledge of the angels. I dove into my Bible with every concordance I own and the Bible program on my computer. I found 273 Scriptures with the words *angels* or *angel* in them, plus many more Scripture references from the words or phrases *heavenly host(s), Gabriel, Michael, archangel,* etc.

Obviously, there are many references to angels throughout the Bible (see the references listed in the back of this book). The Scriptures give us a vast amount of information about the duties of the angels and how we can utilize their abilities for our good.

Nevertheless, there are also references that can be misinterpreted when read out of context. We must be careful to get correct information and gain knowledge. We must then pray for wisdom and discernment so we will utilize that knowledge for our best interest and the betterment of those around us.

Over the past few years, I have read and talked with many leading Christian men and women who have researched and written about the subject of angels. It has never been my intent to put the angels in a position to be worshiped. Rather, by endeavoring to gain as much knowledge as possible on the subject of angels, it has helped me see their true identity, reason for creation, and relationship to us on this earth.

A commonly used verse to explain the relative positions of men and angels is Psalm 8:5, *"For Thou hast made him* [man, humankind] *a little lower than the angels, and hast crowned him with glory and honour."* (KJV). This would imply that angels are of a higher order than man. But actually, the word for *angel* in this verse is *Elohim*, which translates to mean "God" (Hebrew language). This gives us a much clearer perspective of where we stand and where the angels stand with the Father God.

It is sometimes helpful to look at another Bible translation to get a clear understanding of a Scripture. The *Amplified* translation of Psalm 8:5 reads, *"Yet You have made him but a little lower than God [or heavenly beings], and You have crowned him with glory and honor."*

Let's see what Revelation 22:9 says about our relationship to angels.

> *But he said to me, Refrain! [You must not do that!] I am [only] a fellow servant along with yourself and with your brethren the prophets and with those who are mindful of and practice [the truths contained in] the messages of this book. Worship God!*

In this passage of Scripture the angel calls himself a fellow servant with man. If the angels were of a higher order than man, then they couldn't be fellow servants. *Fellow servant* means to be equal, or on the same level.

In fact, First Corinthians 6:3 says, *"Do you not know also that we [Christians] are to judge the [very] angels and pronounce opinion between right and wrong [for them]?"* Obviously, the angels are not above us in rank, or we would not be given the authority to judge them.

The angels are supernatural beings and have tremendous power to do great and mighty works. This is all true. But the point that I am making is that they are not above us in relationship with the Father God. In fact, in many ways you could make the case for just the opposite, that we are above angels in our relationship with God. When we accept Jesus Christ as our Lord and Savior, we then have the right and privilege to become "one spirit" with the Father God. *"But the person who is united to the Lord becomes one spirit with Him"* (1 Cor. 6:17). Ephesians 4:4 says there is *"one body and one Spirit—just as there is also one hope [that belongs] to the calling you received."* We are given "sonship" through the spirit of adoption and the blood of the Lamb:

> For [the Spirit which] you have now received [is] not a spirit of slavery to put you once more in bondage to fear, but you have received the Spirit of adoption [the Spirit producing sonship] in [the bliss of] which we cry, Abba (Father)! Father! (Romans 8:15)

Based on the Scriptures, here is how I see the rank of authority through relationship in God's Word. [Please note this is *my* opinion based on the extensive scriptural research I have done. You should never just accept any man's (or woman's) opinion as truth.

Study the Scriptures yourself and ask the Lord to give you revelation of His Word.]

First level—God, the Father; God, the Son; God, the Holy Spirit

Second level—angels and man

Third level—creatures of all kinds and satan and demons

No one can be on the level with the Godhead. Therefore, Father-Son-Holy Spirit are three in one on this level of top authority.

The second level would have to be created beings with great spiritual abilities and God's image (humankind), since God himself gave us authority.

*God said, Let Us [Father, Son, and Holy Spirit] make mankind in Our image, after Our likeness, and let them have complete authority over the fish of the sea, the birds of the air, the [tame] beasts, and over all of the earth, and over everything that creeps upon the earth. So God created man in His own image, in the image and likeness of God He created him; male and female He created them (Genesis 1:26-27).*

Why would satan and his demons be on the third level with the animals? They were once angels and on the second level with the angels. But then satan made a detrimental choice and one-third of the angels chose to follow him. Satan's basic sin was that of unchecked personal ambition, desiring to be equal to or above God. Satan's fall was occasioned by two things: pride that presumed to supplant God's rule with his own and self-will that asserted independence from the Most High.[1]

> *You were the anointed cherub that covers with overshadowing [wings], and I set you so. You were upon the holy mountain of God; you walked up and down in the midst of the stones of fire [like the paved work of gleaming sapphire stone upon which the God of Israel walked on Mount Sinai].*

> *You were blameless in your ways from the day you were created until iniquity and guilt were found in you.*

> *Through the abundance of your commerce you were filled with lawlessness and violence, and you sinned; therefore I cast you out as a profane thing from the mountain of God and the guardian cherub drove you out from the midst of the stones of fire.*

> *Your heart was proud and lifted up because of your beauty; you corrupted your wisdom for the sake of your splendor. I cast you to the ground; I lay you before kings, that they might gaze at you* (Ezekiel 28:14-17).

> *How have you fallen from heaven, O light-bringer and daystar, son of the morning! How you have been cut down to the ground, you who weakened and laid low the nations [O blasphemous, satanic king of Babylon!]*

> *And you said in your heart, I will ascend to heaven; I will exalt my throne above the stars of God; I will sit upon the mount of assembly in the uttermost north.*

> *I will ascend above the heights of the clouds; I will make myself like the Most High.*

*Yet you shall be brought down to Sheol (Hades), to the innermost recesses of the pit (the region of the dead).*

*Those who see you will gaze at you and consider you, saying, Is this the man who made the earth tremble, who shook kingdoms?—who made the world like a wilderness and overthrew its cities, who would not permit his prisoners to return home?* (Isaiah 14:12-17)

Satan and one-third of the angels tried to steal God's glory, an action that always brings destruction. This, by the way, is why satan wants to get you operating in pride, which is his counterfeit for God's glory. God's Word says in Proverbs 16:18, *"Pride goes before destruction, and a haughty spirit before a fall"* (NKJV). Satan and the one-third of the angels who followed him lost the authority they already had. The Bible says they were thrown out of Heaven and cast down (see Ezek. 28:17).

When you are cast down you have to go below where you once were. There was only one other level to go down to, and that is with the dogs! Satan and all of his demons are on the level of rights and authority with the animals. Remember, in Genesis 1:26 we are given *"complete authority over the fish of the sea, the birds of the air, the [tame] beasts, and over all of the earth, and over everything that creeps upon the earth."* The devil and his cohorts certainly creep around like lions looking for whom they may devour, but God has given us complete authority over them!

Angels and humans are referred to as "sons of God" 66 times throughout the Bible. In the following Scriptures, angels are referred to as "sons of God."

*Now there was a day when the sons (the angels) of God came to present themselves before the Lord, and Satan (the adversary and accuser) also came among them* (Job 1:6).

*Again there was a day when the sons of God [the angels] came to present themselves before the Lord, and Satan (the adversary and the accuser) came also among them to present himself before the Lord* (Job 2:1).

*When the morning stars sang together and all the sons of God shouted for joy?* (Job 38:7)

In Romans 8:14 men are referred to as "sons of God": *"For all who are led by the Spirit of God are sons of God."* Hosea also uses that expression:

*Yet the number of the children of Israel shall be as the sand of the sea, which cannot be measured or numbered; and instead of it being said to them, You are not My people, it shall be said to them, Sons of the Living God!* (Hosea 1:10)

This is further proof to me that in God's sight humans and angels are on the same level. They are both made reference to with the same phrase, "sons of God."

My point is that humans are not low on the totem pole when it comes to authority with God.

*Then He called His twelve disciples together and gave them power and authority over all demons, and to cure diseases. He sent them to preach the kingdom of God and to heal the sick* (Luke 9:1-2 NKJV).

And Christ commissions us to do the same in Matthew 28:18-20:

THE PRESENCE OF ANGELS IN YOUR LIFE


*...All authority has been given to Me in heaven and on earth. Go therefore and make disciples of all the nations, baptizing them in the name of the Father and of the Son and of the Holy Spirit, teaching them to observe all things that I have commanded you; and lo, I am with you always, even to the end of the age* (NKJV).

Paul also encourages us to *"speak these things, exhort, and rebuke with all authority"* (Titus 2:15 NKJV).

When Jesus is the Lord of our lives, we are joint heirs with Him, adopted into the family of God, grafted into His precious royal family. We must understand our position in Christ! Just listen to this passage of Scripture:

*For you did not receive the spirit of bondage again to fear, but you received the Spirit of adoption by whom we cry out, "Abba, Father." The Spirit Himself bears witness with our spirit that we are children of God, and if children, then heirs—heirs of God and joint heirs with Christ, if indeed we suffer with Him, that we may also be glorified together* (Romans 8:15-17 NKJV).

Wow! We are adopted as God's children to receive His inheritance—we are His beneficiaries!

God's Word also calls us a chosen generation, a royal priesthood, a holy nation.

*But you are a chosen generation, a royal priesthood, a holy nation, His own special people, that you may proclaim the praises of Him who called you out of darkness into His marvelous light* (1 Peter 2:9 NKJV).

The word *chosen* designates one picked out from among the larger group for special service or privileges. It describes Christ as the chosen Messiah of God in Luke 23:35:

> *And the people stood looking on. But even the rulers with them sneered, saying, "He saved others; let Him save Himself if He is the Christ, the chosen of God"* (NKJV).

It describes angels as messengers from Heaven:

> *I solemnly charge you in the presence of God and of Christ Jesus and of the chosen angels that you guard and keep [these rules] without personal prejudice or favor, doing nothing from partiality...* (I Timothy 5:21 AMP).

And it describes believers as recipients of God's favor.

> *And unless those days were shortened, no flesh would be saved; but for the elect's sake those days will be shortened* (Matthew 24:22 NKJV).

> *Who shall bring a charge against God's elect? It is God who justifies* (Romans 8:33 NKJV).

> *Therefore, as the elect of God, holy and beloved, put on tender mercies, kindness, humility, meekness, longsuffering* (Colossians 3:12 NKJV).

The words *chosen* and *elect* are used interchangeably throughout the Scriptures, depending on which Bible we study. The Amplified uses the word *chosen*. The NKJV uses the word *elect* in most instances.

The New Testament traces the source of election (being chosen) to God's grace.[2] By God's grace, we have authority through the blood of Jesus that is mighty and powerful. It is time we find our God-given position and get in it! The angels are created to help us on the earth, but if we don't know how to use what God has given us, it won't do us much good!

Hebrews 1:14 is the best revelation of position between angels and man. It says:

> Are not the angels all ministering spirits (servants) sent out in the service [of God for the assistance] of those who are to inherit salvation?

That's you and me! We are to inherit salvation through Jesus. I am learning more about my position in Jesus. I don't want to perish for lack of knowledge. Through God's grace and provision, I want to succeed for God's Kingdom and in His service!

## ENDNOTES

1. Jack W. Hayford, exec. ed., *Spirit-Filled Life Bible* (Nashville: Thomas Nelson, 1991), Commentary, 981.

2. Ibid., Word Wealth, 1910.

# 21

# NEITHER MALE NOR FEMALE

We are all children of God—Period! Gender isn't
of importance in eternity. When God looks at us,
He looks at our spirit man. If our goal is to spend
eternity with the Father, once we get there, our
gender here on earth won't matter at all.

— *Harry Salem II*

In the last chapter we concluded from God's Word that we are
"sons" and "heirs" of God. Galatians 3:26-28 says it all for me:

> *For you are all sons of God through faith in Christ Jesus. For
> as many of you as were baptized into Christ have put on Christ.
> There is neither Jew nor Greek, there is neither slave nor free,
> there is neither male nor female; for you are all one in Christ
> Jesus* (NKJV).

Paul is saying that in Christ there are no distinctions of race, rank, and gender that either hinder fellowship or grant special privileges.

I wish that we, as the Body of Christ, could all be so impartial. James 3:17 says that one of the qualities of wisdom from above is being *without* partiality.

> *But the wisdom that is from above is first pure, then peaceable, gentle, willing to yield, full of mercy and good fruits, without partiality and without hypocrisy* (NKJV).

Let me tell you a fantastic story that changed my perspective about who I am in Christ. I had been in full-time ministry since 1980, and during those years I had experienced many different types of stereotyping in the Body of Christ. Many times it would come from within me and my own limited thinking. More than once I have questioned God and even, at times, almost argued with Him about something He was asking me to do. I have found myself saying to God, "But, God, I am just a girl. I can't go in there and say that! What would people think?"

Nothing was more exciting or revealing than the story I am about to share with you. It changed my own thinking about who I am in Christ and what I am capable of doing through Christ who strengthens me.

I was ministering in Kissimmee, Florida. The pastor's wife hosted a monthly women's luncheon at the church, and I was the speaker. I was sharing on the subject of self-image and talking about who we are in Christ. I was using Genesis 1:26-27 as my Scripture reference. I had all the ladies read it out loud with me. We read,

*God said, Let Us [Father, Son, and Holy Spirit] make mankind in Our image, after Our likeness, and let them have complete authority over the fish of the sea, the birds of the air, the [tame] beasts, and over all of the earth, and over everything that creeps upon the earth. So God created man in His own image, in the image and likeness of God He created him; male and female He created them.*

I pointed out to all the women that we are not left out in the image of God. He made both the male and female and both genders of the species "man" are in the image of God.

Little did I know that the soundman (notice that he was not a she!) didn't believe women should be allowed to minister in the church. Boy, was he in the wrong church for that belief! The pastor of this church continually promotes his wife in ministry, and she is a mighty woman for God. They had women come in to speak at least once a month. God always knows what He is doing!

It had been a marvelous service, and the women were very receptive to God's truth about who we are in Christ. At the close of the service I was singing "Holy Ground," as I usually do in preparation for the ministry time. As I was singing, a lady in the front row fell back in her seat as if she was touched by the power of the Holy Spirit.

The Holy Spirit who dwells within me spoke to my heart and said that He had nothing to do with this woman's lapse of consciousness—in other words, this woman wasn't being touched by God at that moment! There was a nurse sitting close by the now unconscious woman. The Lord moved on the heart of this nurse to get up and go check on the woman. The nurse leaned over the lady and searched for a pulse, felt for breath, and listened for a heartbeat. I was continuing to sing "Holy Ground" as I walked down the steps of the platform to the floor of the auditorium where the ladies were all seated.

The nurse couldn't find any signs of life. She looked up at me, as I was making my way down the altar steps, and shook her head. I just continued to sing "Holy Ground." I didn't panic and, praise God, the anointing was very strong.

As I neared the lady, the Holy Spirit began to tell me how to deal with this situation. (I didn't have any idea what I was going to do when I left the platform, but God gave me instruction exactly when I needed it.)

I stopped singing and took my mike away from my mouth. The track continued to play the music to "Holy Ground." I laid my hands on the woman and commanded her to live and not die. Psalm 118:17 says, *"I shall not die, but live, and declare the works of the Lord"* (NKJV).

I commanded the spirit of death to leave her and the spirit of life to come back into her in the name of Jesus. *"For the law of the Spirit of life in Christ Jesus has made me free from the law of sin and death"* (Rom. 8:2 NKJV).

I knew that I was walking out the Scripture in Second Timothy 1:7, *"God hath not given us the spirit of fear; but of power, and of love, and of a sound mind"* (KJV). For as I said these simple words of faith and rebuked the demonic force that had tried to steal her life, the lady sat straight up in her chair and said, "Where am I?"

I told her she was in church, and I continued to sing the rest of the song. I told the congregation later that if that woman wanted to die and go on and be with Jesus that was just fine with me, but not here today. I didn't want the reputation in the ministry of having people die in my services!

Great story? This is not the end of the story. In fact, it's not even the point! God had a much greater lesson to teach through this incident. That God can raise people from the dead was proven throughout His Word. And that we can do what He did while He was on the earth is also completely spelled out in His Word in John 14:12-13:

> *Most assuredly, I say to you, he who believes in Me, the works that I do he will do also; and greater works than these he will do, because I go to My Father. And whatever you ask in My name, that I will do, that the Father may be glorified in the Son* (NKJV).

The point that God was making was not so blatant. You have to look like the Father does, from the beginning to the end, to get it all! Remember the soundman who didn't think women should teach in church? Well, God made a point with him that would minister deeply to me as well.

While all of this was going on, my traveling companion was sitting with him in the balcony. As I began to walk off the platform toward the lady in distress, the Lord let this soundman have a glimpse into the spirit realm to teach him a life-changing lesson.

After the service the soundman was brought to me and his countenance *and attitude* were completely different than when we had sound checked before the service. He began to tell me that when the lady fell back in her chair and I began to leave the platform, his own eyes were opened to another dimension. He said that as I walked toward the woman seated in the audience, I began to grow right before his eyes. As he was looking right at me, I grew taller and taller and larger and larger, bursting out with muscles. My neck, arms, legs—everywhere on my body was covered with muscles. He said my muscles had muscles! By the time I reached the woman, he could hardly believe his eyes. He said, "You were *huge!*" Being a woman, normally I might have been offended for someone to say that I was "huge," but in this instance I was elated!

The soundman began to question God about what he was seeing, what was happening, and what it all meant. God began to tell him. God said to him that in the spirit realm we are neither male nor female; we are only *weak* or *strong* in Christ. The devil sees our spirit "man" or spirit being, not our flesh. If our spirit man is well fed and nourished, it will be strong and healthy and will put the devil on the run. However, if our spirit is starved from a lack of praying and studying God's Word, we will be puny and weak, and the devil will not be intimidated. God allowed the soundman to see what the devil sees (and what God sees).

My spirit is well fed, so I am dangerous to the devil. It doesn't matter whether I am a female or a male. It only matters whether I am strong or weak in Christ. Obviously, from what the soundman saw, I am strong! It's up to me to keep my spirit man that way by what I feed it and how I exercise it. Just as food and exercise help nourish our natural bodies, God's Word and faith (believing God and then acting on it) nourish our spirit man.

This man repented to the Father God for his attitude toward women in ministry, and guess what God did for him that very morning? His unsaved wife was in the audience. During the altar call, she came forward and received Jesus as her Lord and Savior. Praise God!

According to what the soundman saw, my spirit man appeared neither male nor female—just *big!* Jesus says in Luke 20:35-36:

> But those who are counted worthy to attain that age, and the resurrection from the dead, neither marry nor are given in marriage; nor can they die anymore, for they are equal to the angels and are sons of God, being sons of the resurrection (NKJV).

This Scripture says that we (in our resurrected state) will not marry, will not die again, and will be like the angels. Matthew 22:30 says: *"For in the resurrected state neither do [men] marry nor are [women] given in marriage, but they are like the angels in heaven."*

It is obvious from the Scriptures that I have quoted that angels do not marry and that we are like them when we get to Heaven. It is also evident that when we are in Heaven and are like the angels, we will no longer be bound by the boundaries of gender.

It stands to reason then that the angels are neither male nor female. The phrase "neither marry nor are given in marriage" leads me to believe that Jesus is referring to male (they marry) and female (they are given in marriage). It seems from what we can gather from the Scriptures that angels are without gender. Gender seems to be of no importance and does not exist in the angelic beings.

Even though they may not actually be male or female, the angels can appear to be different. Yet, when I have seen the angels, they have appeared to be men. They all took on the appearance of the male gender. Throughout the Bible, the angels that have appeared to different ones upon the earth seemed to be male also.

There is only one reference to angelic heavenly beings in the entire Bible that alludes to them appearing female—in Zechariah 5:9:

*Then lifted I up my eyes and looked, and behold, there were two women coming forward! The wind was in their wings, for they had wings like the wings of a stork, and they lifted up the ephah[-sized vessel] between the earth and the heavens.*

I want you to notice that I am continually using the words *appear, appeared, appearing.* Since angels do not reproduce, gender would not be necessary. It seems that angels take on whatever appearance is necessary to accomplish the tasks that they are given by the Father God.

Angels are not human. They are heavenly beings—and they can talk. They are vehicles, messengers, a means to an end for the Father God. God made plenty of them, so reproduction is not necessary. They have no gender. We must not think of angels as human beings. Take the limits off your thinking. They are spirit. Try to think like God—not so human!

In our spiritual state of being, we have no gender either. I am not a female spirit who can reproduce other little spirits. No! That would be impossible. God's Word is very specific that in our spiritual states of being we do not marry, reproduce, or have gender.

I have been so thankful for this revelation through God's Word in my life as a minister of the Gospel. Unfortunately, many people tend to judge all of us on our humanness and not on our spiritual abilities.

God made you either male or female on this earth for a reason. So, thank Him for whatever gender He has made you, and enjoy the gender that you are.

Now, males and females, I want to ask you a question. Are you a threat to the devil, or is he unmoved by your spirit man? You must feed your spirit man to become the man or woman that God has called and created you to be. Are you strong? Are you weak? How do the demons see you?

I pray your spirit man will grow and come forth in the boldness, power, and authority of Jesus Christ.

# 22

## ONLY BETTER IN HEAVEN

I know. I know. I said in the last chapter that gender won't matter when we get to Heaven. And I know that's right. It's just that I love Cheryl so much I can't imagine not being her husband. But God's Word is true, and I know by His promise that I will be with Cheryl and my children for eternity. And our relationship won't be the same as it is here on earth—it will be better! Thank God! Look what we have to look forward to!

Cheryl and I are alike in many ways and different in many more, but iron sharpens iron and that is why we wrote this book this way—to present different perspectives. When it comes to the subject of gender in Heaven, I'll leave that up to her interpretation. Thinking about humans and angels having no gender in Heaven isn't really the issue with me because I never think of my Savior or God beingofonegenderortheotherbutratherhaving a strength, a power, something supernatural. I think the rub comes with Cheryl when earthly mindedpeopleportrayangelsaschildlike,baby cherubs—something weak. I don't believe, nor doesCheryl,thatanythingdealingwithourGod is weak. Only man is weak.

— *Harry Salem II*

The subject of being married in Heaven has been discussed in our home in great detail since the onset of our studies of the spiritual realm. My precious husband, Harry, just doesn't like the idea that we will not be married in Heaven! I get tickled and laugh at the look on his face when we discuss this subject!

It's only human nature for us to want things that are good in our lives to go on being that way for all of eternity, and I believe that they will. In fact, in Heaven they will be even better! We learned from the last chapter that we will neither marry nor be given in marriage (see Matt. 22:30). The way Jesus phrased that verse seems to indicate that we will be genderless in Heaven or, at the very least, we won't have flesh—therefore, no need to "satisfy" the flesh since we won't have any—"earthly" flesh, that is.

We have already discussed in past chapters Scriptures that give us clarity on the subjects of gender, reproduction, and marriage in the heavenly sphere. The angels are immortal and they do not marry, and we will be like the angels.

I believe that I will be with my husband, children, parents, and family who are in Heaven. I believe that we will be together but without the restrictions and prejudices of gender, age, time, and humanness. What a marvelous place Heaven must be! All love, no hate. All peace, no strife. All joy, no sorrow. It's more than the human brain can comprehend! Why? Because God's ways are unsearchable!

> *Oh, the depth of the riches both of the wisdom and knowledge of God! How unsearchable are His judgments and His ways past finding out!* (Romans 11:33 NKJV)

That's why we must accept it all by faith, knowing that our Father God will only do those things that are beneficial for us. We are not limited by anything—no gender, race, creed, financial status, nothing with limits!

Angels have no need for marriage because they were all created by God. They are not born. As I said in the last chapter, there is no reproduction in angelic beings. And contrary to popular belief, there is no such thing as a baby angel. There may be babies in Heaven, but they are not angels.

Yet the world's portrayal of angels is as tiny, fat, winged creatures called *cherubs.* That is a nice thought or idea, but there is no Scripture to support such a belief.

Before you think I'm cynical, I'm not telling you to get rid of these types of "what-nots" in your homes. They are sweet and remind us of God's interventions on the earth just by the sight of them. But we should always be as well-learned and versed as we possibly can on any subject that has to do with God. The truth is vitally important in keeping ourselves from deception.

Apparently, angels don't age or decay like we humans do. This is evidenced in Luke 20:36: *"Nor can they die anymore, for they are equal to the angels and are sons of God, being sons of the resurrection"* (NKJV).

They appear to be of a vibrant "age," somewhere between 20 and 40 by human measurements of time and age. I believe from what I can gather from the Scriptures that when they were created, they were of this same exact age and description. The angel Gabriel appeared four times throughout the Bible with thousands of years between visits, and it doesn't seem that he aged or changed in appearance.

I want to address one last question on the subject of angels being genderless. If the angels have no gender, then how can the "sons of God" lie with the daughters of men and produce giants in the land? Interesting question, isn't it?

> *The sons of God saw the daughters of men, that they were beauti-*
> *ful; and they took wives for themselves of all whom they chose....*
> *There were giants on the earth in those days, and also afterward,*
> *when the sons of God came in to the daughters of men and they*
> *bore children to them* (Genesis 6:2,4 NKJV).

As we studied earlier, when the angels that rebelled with satan were thrown out of Heaven, they became lower than man, on the same level of authority with the animals. Satan hated this. I believe satan caused the demons to take on the shape or appearance of mankind (remember that the angels did this all the time through-out the Bible). The NKJV *Spirit-Filled Life Bible* commentary says that the "sons of God" in Genesis 6:2 may have been angels who rebelliously left Heaven to take women as wives.[1]

Maybe satan thought that through his demons he could pro-duce a race of people apart from God, with the help of the female reproductive system. Satan would then have his own beings and take some of God's people with him at the same time. You may say, "Cheryl, that's pretty far-fetched." It may well be, and this is only my own supposition, but we know from the sin nature and observing society that sex is one of satan's greatest weapons when it is perverted.

We must never forget why satan was kicked out of Heaven in the first place. He wanted to be like God. He wanted to be God. He wanted the angels to worship him instead of the only true God. Satan tries to take things that God has made that are beautiful and corrupt them. I believe this is what he did in that Scripture in Genesis.

The demons took on the fleshly appearance of men, then lay with women, impregnating them, producing giants on the earth. All the angels that I have seen and many that are written about in the Bible are very large. The combination of human and angelic (fallen angels) beings through sex caused abnormal reproduction—thus producing giants.

Isn't it interesting to contemplate the details of the angels through Scripture? There are so many things that aren't "spelled out" in the Scriptures. Sometimes that is because we don't need to know everything. Trust is based on not knowing all the answers and still believing. Think about this. In our glorified heavenly bodies, there will be no prejudice against gender or color or creed or nationality or anything else. We will all be one in spirit with God.

Maybe you don't like the idea of not being male or female in Heaven. If I turn out to be a "female" glorified body, that will be great; but it doesn't matter, because in Heaven no one will be better or worse, higher or lower, richer or poorer. I will be so glad just to be in His presence and to worship Him in Spirit and truth. God wants only the absolute best for us. It's going to be abundantly better there!

The Bible says that we will be known in Heaven as we are known on the earth. I am known here as a female, but "female" in itself is for reproduction, which will not happen or be necessary in Heaven. I am known here as Harry's wife; Harry III, Roman, and Gabrielle's mother; Hosea and Carrie Prewitt's daughter; Miss America 1980; and many more descriptions. Being male or female is not so much about gender as it is about who we actually are within our being.

When the Bible says we won't marry, or be given in marriage, then it is more in reference to gender function, not how we are known, so relax! Most of all and above all else, I want to be known as a worshiper and bride of Christ. How about you?

## ENDNOTE

1. Jack W. Hayford, exec. ed., *Spirit-Filled Life Bible* (Nashville: Thomas Nelson, 1991), Commentary, 14.

# 23

## Warriors: But Not Always Active Combat

Every situation in life is one that God ordains for us. We have to learn from every situation and not take anything for granted, especially the angels. One thing I can tell you about Cheryl: when she's bothered by something in her spirit, she won't quit until she gets an answer from the Lord. Thank God she didn't quit this time. The experience you'll read about in this chapter changed us forever. When Cheryl and I are going to speak or preach for a two- or three-day weekend of services, we prepare spiritually at least one full week before and one full week after. And that's a fact! We are in spiritual combat. You are, too. Be prepared and don't be a casualty of war!

— *Harry Salem* II

There was one church crusade we attended during the summer of 1992 that was uniquely significant. The angels were present in the services, but their actions were totally different from any other services. Because of the lessons learned, I feel it is important to share the events of the weekend with you.

During the crusade the people were so gracious and kind to us. The pastors are dear friends of ours, and we were expecting great services. The worship team was really excited because of the previous services. There had been so many wonderful works of God, plus, the intervention of the angels in each service added to the level of expectation and excitement. We were on a natural "high" in anticipation of great things. We were all chattering and laughing and having a great, fun time.

As the first service began, there was something different in the air. It seemed harder somehow to get into the praise and worship that had been so natural in other services. I was constantly looking for the angels and some sign of activity in the spirit realm.

The church pastors, church staff, and congregation were all wonderful. Yet the flow of anointing was stifled and stiff compared to the other services. I was still anticipating the angels. I gave my testimony and sang songs of praise unto the Father God. The worship team had already led in worship, and the people entered into the singing, but something was missing. Something...I just wasn't sure what.

I was looking toward the podium when I noticed out of the corner of my eye the angels coming into the building. This time, instead of the angels coming into the sanctuary with tremendous flurry, the sounds of thousands of beings entering all at the same time—they came in slowly, quietly, and somewhat passively.

There were empty seats on the floor section of the church, and the balcony was almost completely empty. The angels began filling the unused seats in the balcony, and some of the angels sat among the people on the floor section in the empty seats.

I couldn't understand the atmosphere that I was perceiving. They seemed to be totally uninterested in the events of the service. There was no excitement among any of them. This was such a contrast to their reactions at previous meetings that I just couldn't get a grip on what I was seeing and feeling.

The angels were almost "lounging" around! They laid their weapons down on the seats beside them. They lay down in the balcony with their legs stretched out in front of them, ankles crossed, and arms folded behind their heads. Many of the angels were yawning and seemed to fall asleep.

They showed no interest in the service, and I could hardly believe what I was seeing! They were apparently relaxed and seemed unconcerned about the events that were taking place. The best word I could come up with as I thought back on it was *complacent.* They just didn't seem to care about what, if anything, was going on in this service.

They were dressed like before. In fact, their appearance showed no change at all. They were still 10 to 12 feet tall, with massive muscles and beautifully defined physiques. They had their weapons, a few were carrying trumpets, some were showing their wings, and others were not. They appeared only as white light. There were no color variations as I had seen on other occasions. Everything looked as before, but there was definitely a big difference. They weren't doing anything. Nothing! They just sat there doing nothing!

As the service progressed, some of the angels got up and changed seats. But even this movement didn't show any signs of enthusiasm. There was absolute lethargy in the air. They reminded me of a scene on a lazy Sunday afternoon after a huge dinner. You know, the kind of afternoon where everyone just hangs around and takes naps because they are too full to move. That's what they looked like!

If the angels were sitting up, their backsides were slouched down in their seats; their heads were lying on the backs of the seats, their hair cascading over the padded pew. Their eyes wandered around as if they were bored with this whole thing, and their knees were propped up on the seats in front of them. It was a sight!

During the service I didn't know what to think. I was dumb-founded! I was grasping at straws trying to explain to my rational mind what was taking place. I thought that maybe there was so much prayer cover that the angels didn't have much to do during the service. This seemed to be a reasonable explanation, and certainly one that I wanted to accept.

After the first night's service ended, we met in the pastor's study for refreshments. I began telling those present what I had seen during the service, and everyone seemed to agree with me that the prayer cover must be the answer to the relaxed attitudes of the angels.

The gifts of the Holy Spirit had flowed during the service. People had responded rather slowly, but they still responded. Even though there had not been a huge number of people healed, saved, and set free—still all those things had happened to some degree. So God had obviously blessed this meeting.

As Harry and I went back to our hotel room, I just couldn't get a peace in my spirit about any of the service, the angels' obvious lack of concern, or my explanation of the angels' actions. I lay awake all night and analyzed the situation over and over with a restlessness in my soul.

Finally, as morning approached, the answer came so vividly. It was not that there was too much prayer cover at all! It was much bigger than that. If anything, it was the opposite of too much. We, as a team, had gotten so accustomed to the glorious move of the Spirit of God that we were expecting the exact type of "flow" in the Spirit that had been evidenced before. We expected the angels to come fight the demons of darkness and to see miracles flow automatically.

What we expected was obvious. What we got was a great big surprise. The lack of action on the angels' parts was a direct result of *not enough prayer*, instead of too much! We were anticipating great things, we were looking, laughing, having a wonderful Holy Ghost time. But what we weren't doing was *praying!* We had relaxed and forgotten to pray at all!

So many times we talk about prayer, but how often is it just that? Talk...not prayer. We had talked all right, but we had not prayed. So we got serious as a team. We organized a group to go to the church hours before the service and march around the grounds, pray in the Spirit, and pray in understanding. Another group was set up to enter the building and pray and intercede for the following evening's service. The rest were to pray as they went about their daily duties at the church.

We were praying again. We were in harmony and unity, working for a common goal in the Spirit of God. We wanted things to be different in this evening's service. Yet, it was still difficult—it was hard to concentrate as we prayed. Every little thing distracted our attention from our goal to pray. We continued to pray, but it was like "pulling teeth" in the spirit realm.

I would love to tell you there was a great breakthrough that evening. But that would not be the truth. We did see a slight change in the service. There were more miracles, more salvations, and more of the move of God. But it wasn't easy! It was not "fun" at all for any of us. It was hard work.

From that time until now, we never take it for granted that there will be a great move of God at any meeting. We begin to pray fervently days before each service. There must be time spent getting prepared for the services—not just our sermons prepared, but our spirits prepared for war. Dark spiritual walls must begin to crumble over a city before we get there. The angels must be dispatched before we even get to the city. The angels have preparation work to do, just as we have prepared ourselves to be there and hear the voice of the Father God. Then we pray for several days after each service to protect the miracles and blessings that were given by God.

We also encourage the churches to activate intercessory prayer teams to pray before, during, and after the services. We know from our own experiences that a church that has constant, true intercession has a different spirit around it than one that does not pray.

Evidence from the Scriptures reveals that certain demons are assigned over certain territories in our world. And there are prevalent happenings in different parts of the country that must be more than just mere coincidence. Many theologians have speculated about the "prince of Persia" in the Book of Daniel being a demonic prince. The "prince of Persia" withstood the angel Gabriel for 21 days and kept him from getting to Daniel, who had been praying and fasting, seeking an answer.

The archangel Michael had to come and help Gabriel fight his way through the heavenlies so that Gabriel could deliver the Lord's answer to Daniel's fervent prayers. It stands to reason that the "prince of Persia" was a dark spiritual being who was opposing God's angels and trying to stop them from accomplishing their missions.

I don't claim to have any special knowledge in this area of territorial spirits. All I know is what I have experienced in the many years I have traveled all over the world. There is a different attitude in people from different regions in a country. There are different things that seem generally "wrong" in an area. (Remember what the Lord showed me about the Midwestern town whose claim to fame was a famous author who was an atheist?)

Certain areas may deal with the sin of pornography, while another area may have a large percentage of their population who attend church but who don't seem to produce any fruit. In other words, they don't "walk the talk" of their Christianity during the rest of the week. Still another area may have a tremendously high crime rate. I don't believe it is just coincidence that these similar things happen in a designated area. I really don't think that "it's in the water." I tend to think that there are certain demons who are assigned to certain areas, cities, regions, or territories that cause these similar problems within the minds, bodies, and spirits of the inhabitants.

I am not sure what we were battling in that town. But I am sure of one thing. We had gotten too comfortable and had not diligently prayed. And even after much prayer, there was not the breakthrough in the spiritual realm that we expected and wanted. There were problems in the heavenlies that a few hours of prayer would not change. There needed to be determined and consistent intercession to bombard and dismantle whatever was holding that church, city, or even possibly...that territory.

# 24

## THIS CROWN ONLY COMES WITH A PRICE!

The summer of 1992 was one neither Cheryl nor I will ever forget. There was glory and there was tragedy. There was an increase in faith and the manifestation of miracles, and there was a testing and purging that seemed too much to bear at times. Cheryl was seeing the angels, and our whole family was paying the price right along with her. There were times when I actually said to her, "Cheryl, it's those angels—why do you have to keep seeing those angels?" But as I look back and reflect on all that followed, I believe the Lord allowed Cheryl to see the angels to help her through the seven months she had to spend flat on her back and then the year or more of total exhaustion and sickness that almost took her life and mine, too.

You see, God had a plan for Cheryl and for me, but there was a price we both had to pay before we would be ready to move into His perfect will and plan. He had a crown, very different from the glittering Miss America crown, that He wanted Cheryl and me both to wear. For Cheryl this meant letting go of the driven need to strive for perfection and the pride of performance, learning to find rest in the Lord, and learning to trust me to be her spiritual covering as God intends for a husband to be. For me, it meant dying to self (that was huge!) and learning "how" to be that spiritual covering for Cheryl.

I'll let Cheryl fill you in on more of the details, but I want you to know Harry Salem is a new man in Christ Jesus today. People who know me will tell you that before all this took place, my office was the one no one wanted to walk into. And God knows, they sure didn't want me to walk into theirs! When they used the term "mean as a snake," that was me. But you don't know how mean a snake is, because no one wants to be around one. I was the best father, but I was hard on my wife and especially hard on people at work.

Through these past four or five years, God has burned out the chaff and taught me about His lovingkindness and how to have a relationship with Him. Now He is sending Cheryl and me out to teach other couples how to find this loving relationship with Him and with each other. I

believethisisthecrownHewantedustowear,and
I'm glad we chose to pay the price. What Cheryl
and I have gained has been worth it all. No longer
isthereCherylorHarry.Nowit'stheSalems—one
in the Lord and one in marriage.

— *Harry Salem II*

During 1992 the angelic visitations were numerous. By the end of the summer, I had seen them fill a big convention center in Tulsa. I had seen them in Buffalo, New York; New Orleans, Louisiana; and Los Angeles, California. They had roamed our home and spoken to me more than once. They had shown me protection and direction, and they had given me messages for others.

It was a glorious time, but I soon began to realize that with the glory comes persecution. And nobody wants to hear that. When people tell me they want to see angels, I always ask them, "Are you ready to walk into that supernatural realm and everything else that comes with it?" Luke 12:48 says, "*...For everyone to whom much is given, from him much will be required; and to whom much has been committed, of him they will ask the more*" (NKJV).

Harry and I had to walk this Scripture out in the months and years after I began to see the angels. Now let me give you a brief glimpse into what we walked through and how our Father God used it for our good.

I first saw the angels in Buffalo, New York, in early June of 1992. In July we miscarried our precious baby, Malachi Charles. However, the Lord restored what the enemy had stolen, and we became pregnant again early that fall. In November, the strain of travel and ministry took its toll. There were complications with the pregnancy, and the doctor ordered me to bed for the remaining seven months of my pregnancy with Gabrielle.

Once I hit the bed, the frequency of seeing the angels stopped. It was just God and me. Harry will tell you that making me stay in bed was like putting King Kong in a cage! I couldn't wait for everyone to go to school and to work so I could get up out of that bed. Harry knew when he called if the phone rang more than once, I was not in bed where I belonged. That's how rebellious I was.

Harry tried to channel my pent-up energy into writing a book about our children. It seemed like a good idea, but when I would pick up my pen and paper, the only words that would come were, "Why is it when you are in crisis you can't create?" No matter what I tried to do, I couldn't accomplish a thing. I became angry and frustrated. (Oh, I wasn't nice to live with at all.) But God was able to get my attention, and He made sure He got it.

All my life I had always wanted approval, always wanted to do good, always wanted to save the world from what I'd been through. God had rescued me, and I thought I had to rescue everybody else. I know now that the abuse I suffered when I was a child had planted seeds of unworthiness that caused me to seek approval at all cost. The problem was, I was trying to do it my way. No matter what I did, even becoming Miss America, it still wasn't enough. I didn't trust God to do it, and I didn't trust people, not even my husband.

Being in bed all that time was harder than anything I had ever done. I had to learn how to rest in the Lord, and I had no idea how to do it. I thought God wanted me to "do" something about everything that happened. Nothing could just be because He loved *me* or because He cared about *me* or because He wanted to help *me*.

Nothing could be for *me*. It had to be for the world. So I thought I had to save the world all by myself.

At this same time, Harry was going through tremendous stress as well. His blood pressure was high, his cholesterol went up over 500, and he was having chest pain. He was angry at me because I wouldn't behave myself, and he was angry at those angels. He kept saying, "Cheryl, why did you have to see those crazy angels? Are you still seeing them? Well, tell them to get on the job here!" We can laugh about it now, but it wasn't funny at the time.

When I finally came to the end of myself and realized *I* couldn't do anything, the Lord was finally able to get my attention. He told me He just wanted me to learn to rest in Him and give Him all of my attention. He wasn't impressed with *my* agenda. He just wanted to show me that He loved *me* unconditionally.

From that point until Gabrielle was born, I was able to peacefully and joyfully spend my hours studying His Word and worshiping Him. We spent many wonderful hours together in quiet solitude and peace. I learned how to truly find rest in Him and to accept His love for me.

Once Gabrielle was born in May 1993, Harry and I thought we had come through the fire. Little did we know it had only just begun. There was much more pride and "self" the Lord wanted to burn out of us.

A few weeks after birth, Gabrielle was diagnosed with sleep apnea (the condition that causes crib deaths), and a new battle began. Instead of applying what I had learned during my pregnancy about resting in the Lord, I went right back to my old pattern—accepting every ministry date that came along and trying to be "Super Mom" at the same time. It took about three more months of working, traveling, and trying to be a mother to a baby who only slept in short catnaps before it all came crashing down again. My physical body could not take this stress.

All the Lord had taught me in seven months and what Harry had been telling me for years had been pushed aside. I forgot that He said, "Rest in Me." I forgot that He is my only Source. If I had learned my lesson the first time, maybe I could have avoided going through the valley that was ahead. This time He wasn't going to let me get back up until I had truly submitted to Him. I had to learn what complete trust was really all about. The ultimate lesson I had to learn was to trust in the Lord *and* trust in my husband, whom the Lord provided to be my covering.

The next 18 months were a walk through the deepest valley Harry and I had ever experienced. I lost my voice. I was experiencing severe headaches and nausea, and I was losing weight at a drastic rate. The doctors told me I had a multitude of stress-induced problems, including chronic fatigue syndrome and a chemical imbalance in my brain that caused depression. I refused to believe what the doctors were telling me, but I was slipping farther and farther into the valley. I could not help myself. I could not even pray for myself.

You see, I had operated for so long in the supernatural that I tended to ignore the natural. And Harry operated in the natural so much, he couldn't cross over into the supernatural. Now we were bumping heads. I was denying what was happening to my natural body. Harry, who had always provided protection for his family in all the natural ways, such as a security system in the house, for example, suddenly had to start providing a covering in the supernatural realm of prayer, trusting the Lord for my healing, and things of that nature. Our roles had flip-flopped. And neither one of us knew how to function in the circumstances in which we found ourselves.

The battle we fought over the next 18 months was intense. It was life over death. When nothing in the natural seemed to be working, Harry and I *both* turned totally to the Lord to carry us through. When I was too weak to fight for myself, I learned to lean on and to trust my beloved husband and the Lord.

Harry saw me getting weaker and weaker. I was down to 90 pounds. It was then that Harry took a stand and determined that he was not going to allow the enemy (satan) to rob me of my life, to rob him of his wife, or to rob his children of their mother. (Harry's father had died when he was only 10 years old. Now our oldest son was nearing that age, and Harry was not going to allow any generational curse to be continued in this generation.) Harry did what had to be done. He left his full-time position and came home to take care of me and the children.

We literally shut ourselves off from the world for whatever time it took to allow the Lord to heal us totally and completely. We truly learned the meaning of walking out Luke 14:11: *"For whoever exalts himself will be humbled, and he who humbles himself will be exalted"* (NKJV).

We had to humble ourselves daily and give "everything" over to our Father God. Only then was He able to lift us up. When we let go, our Father God took over, and we came out the other side of that valley victoriously praising Him.

We are told over and over throughout His Word that we are not greater than our Master, and that if Jesus was persecuted then we will be also.

*Remember the word that I said to you, 'A servant is not greater than his master.' If they persecuted Me, they will also persecute you. If they kept My word, they will keep yours also* (John 15:20 NKJV).

In the famous Beatitudes, Jesus tells us that the persecuted have a special blessing and will receive the Kingdom of Heaven: *"Blessed are those who are persecuted for righteousness' sake, for theirs is the kingdom of heaven"* (Matt. 5:10 NKJV).

I know this sounds rough—I am not a martyr and I don't like troubles and problems. But there are times when we are surrounded by them, and it seems nothing we can do makes any difference. In those times, I remind myself that everything is for a season and this too shall pass! I love walking in the blessings of God, and I plan to continue until Christ's return. Nevertheless, there may be times when it truly takes my faith to keep walking each step of the way.

I don't want to be so spiritually immature as to think that I will not have to go through trials and tribulations. I must endure all things to become who I am called and created to become. When things begin to overwhelm me, I am encouraged when I remember what happened right after Jesus was baptized. Jesus came up out of the water and God made that beautiful statement about His Son: *"...This is My Son, My Beloved, in Whom I delight!"* (Matt. 3:17).

Then, the Bible tells us clearly what happened immediately thereafter.

*Then Jesus was led (guided) by the [Holy] Spirit into the wilderness (desert) to be tempted (tested and tried) by the devil* (Matthew 4:1).

I wish that the Holy Spirit had not been the One who led Jesus into the desert or wilderness—but the fact is it was the Holy Spirit. It was necessary that Jesus be tempted so that He could resist the devil. It was necessary that He be tempted so that He could defeat the enemy. It proved Jesus' character just as temptation proves our character. It's not so God can see if we will survive. He already knows. It's so we can know our strengths and weaknesses and work on perfecting them through Christ.

We cannot live our lives in fear, dreading horrible things that might await us just around the bend. If we do, we will miss the joy in our journey. God can and will use every trial and temptation to perfect in us His good and perfect will concerning us. God uses what the devil meant for our destruction. He turns it around not just for our good, but also to help us go back and strengthen others—destroying the plans of the enemy!

> *Simon, Simon (Peter), listen! Satan has asked excessively that [all of] you be given up to him [out of the power and keeping of God], that he might sift [all of] you like grain, but I have prayed especially for you [Peter], that your [own] faith may not fail; and when you yourself have turned again, strengthen and establish your brethren (Luke 22:31-32).*

My precious Harry was there for me in my darkest valley. When I couldn't see a way out, he came from behind the scenes, "stepped up to the plate," took over the spiritual covering of our family and began leading us toward victory. I learned to trust him and relax in my rightful (#2) position, knowing that now I can truly blossom into the woman God has called and created me to be.

My once-always-in-the-background husband had come to the forefront and taken not only his rightful position in the family but also his God-given and appointed position in ministry. I always knew God had called Harry to minister with me and me with him, together as a family—an overcoming, victorious family! The devil is defeated and we, the *"violent,"* take it (back) by force in Jesus' name! (see Matt. 11:12).

Harry and I praise our Father God for allowing us to be sifted like grain during those years and we continually thank Jesus for interceding on our behalf. Our faith did not fail in the midst of all the trials. He was faithful and strengthened us so that we are now able to go out and strengthen our sisters and brothers in the faith. Walking in the supernatural and being trusted by the Lord for such discernment requires a price to be paid, but it is truly worth that price. Now we are fulfilling our true destiny for the Father—wearing the crown—seeing lives miraculously changed!

# 25

# Angelic Rank and Order

Cheryl is diligent in researching whatever the Lord shows her. She has spent many hours searching the Scriptures and researching what other biblical experts have to say about God's angels. Take time to study for yourself what the Lord and others have to say on the subject.

The definitions and information in this chapter help us learn that God has ordained everything and that even angels have an order that falls in line with God's plans. Cheryl talks about their military rank and order and this makes sense. We are in the fiercest battle there is, the battle for eternal life. Since the angels are God's warriors, why wouldn't they follow military order? Remember, the battle is the Lord's, and He has already won the final victory. Satan knows his time is short, and his fury is not yet spent. Only God knows the day and the hour

when the last battle will be fought and won. Until
that time, God's angels are fighting on our behalf.

— *Harry Salem II*

Even after I saw the apathetic angels, I have never been fearful of the angels losing any wars to the enemy. I have never been
concerned with God's army not being strong enough or mighty
enough to get the job done for the King of kings and the Lord of
lords. Satan and his demons may bring opposition or delay your
victory, but he ultimately cannot stop it.

It's only by the grace of God that I developed a complete trust
and faith in our Father God even as a child. I decided early on
that if God's Word said it, God meant it. I know God has thought
of everything, and it's not up to me to check His list! So I take it
absolutely to heart when we are given the assurances throughout
God's Word that in the end, we win! The Bible tells us that the
number of angels is innumerable.

> *But rather, you have come to Mount Zion, even to the city of the
> living God, the heavenly Jerusalem, and to countless multitudes
> of angels in festal gathering* (Hebrews 12:22).

> *And suddenly there was with the angel a multitude of the heav-
> enly host praising God...* (Luke 2:13 NKJV).

Only one-third of the angels chose to follow satan and were
cast down from Heaven. That leaves two-thirds of the good angels
to fight for us. Therefore, I do not walk in any fear of the demonic
realm and thoroughly enjoy studying about the angels. Thank
You, Father!

Bible teachers have hashed and rehashed the information that is given throughout the Scriptures on the rank, descriptions of duties, and authority of angels. I can't seem to find any one theory upon which all seem to agree. But it stands to reason that Heaven and the supernatural realm are set up in some type of "governmental" system with different levels of authority. Through the Scriptures we see the words *angels, archangel, seraphim, cherubim, thrones, dominions, principalities* or *rulers, powers* or *authorities*—all listed and made reference to in relationship with heavenly positions, ranks, and job descriptions.

> *For it was in Him that all things were created, in heaven and on earth, things seen and things unseen, whether thrones, dominions, rulers, or authorities; all things were created and exist through Him [by His service, intervention] and in and for Him* (Colossians 1:16).

> *For I am persuaded beyond doubt (am sure) that neither death nor life, nor angels nor principalities, nor things impending and threatening nor things to come, nor powers...will be able to separate us from the love of God...* (Romans 8:38-39).

> *For we are not wrestling with flesh and blood [contending only with physical opponents], but against the despotisms, against the powers, against [the master spirits who are] the world rulers of this present darkness, against the spirit forces of wickedness in the heavenly (supernatural) sphere* (Ephesians 6:12).

Let me familiarize you with a few of the titles applied to angels.

**Angels.** In the New Testament the word has the special sense of a spiritual, heavenly personage attendant upon God and functioning as a messenger from the Lord sent to earth to execute His purposes and make them known to men. Angels are appointed by God to minister to believers.[1]

> *Are not the angels all ministering spirits (servants) sent out in the service [of God for the assistance] of those who are to inherit salvation?* (Hebrews 1:14)

**Archangels.** The word *archangel* means "to be first (in political rank or power)," indicating that this is the highest rank of heavenly hosts. The only archangel specifically mentioned in the Scriptures is Michael.

> *But when [even] the archangel Michael, contending with the devil, judicially argued (disputed) about the body of Moses, he dared not [presume to] bring an abusive condemnation against him, but [simply] said, The Lord rebuke you!* (Jude 1:9)

It will most likely be Michael's shout we will hear at the Second Coming.

> *For the Lord Himself will descend from heaven with a loud cry of summons, with the shout of an archangel, and with the blast of the trumpet of God...* (1 Thessalonians 4:16).

Because Gabriel is prominent in the Bible and also because his name is derived from a root word meaning "strength" or "chief" (politically), which is characteristic of archangels, some conclude that he is also an archangel. This opinion, although not supported by Scripture, was popularized by the poet John Milton.

Many scholars hold that lucifer was an archangel before his fall. However, this is only speculation based on the position and influence he held over the angels who fell with him.[2] Ezekiel 28:12-19 is thought to be a description of lucifer.

*...Thou sealest up the sum, full of wisdom, and perfect in beauty.*

*Thou hast been in Eden the garden of God; every precious stone was thy covering, the sardius, topaz, and the diamond, the beryl, the onyx, and the jasper, the sapphire, the emerald, and the carbuncle, and gold: the workmanship of thy tabrets and of thy pipes was prepared in thee in the day that thou wast created.*

*Thou art the anointed cherub that covereth; and I have set thee so: thou wast upon the holy mountain of God; thou hast walked up and down in the midst of the stones of fire.*

*Thou wast perfect in thy ways from the day that thou wast created, till iniquity was found in thee.*

*By the multitude of thy merchandise they have filled the midst of thee with violence, and thou hast sinned: therefore I will cast thee as profane out of the mountain of God: and I will destroy thee, O covering cherub, from the midst of the stones of fire.*

*Thine heart was lifted up because of thy beauty, thou hast corrupted thy wisdom by reason of thy brightness: I will cast thee to the ground, I will lay thee before kings, that they may behold thee.*

*Thou hast defiled thy sanctuaries by the multitude of thine iniquities, by the iniquity of thy traffick; therefore will I bring forth a fire from the midst of thee, it shall devour thee, and I will bring thee to ashes upon the earth in the sight of all them that behold thee.*

*All they that know thee among the people shall be astonished at thee: thou shalt be a terror, and never shalt thou be any more* (Ezekiel 28:12-19 KJV).

**Seraphim.** The ministry of the seraphim is closely related to the throne and the praises of God. They are seen constantly glorifying God—extolling His nature and attributes, and apparently supervising Heaven's worship. It is possible the seraphim are the praising angels of Psalm 148:2, though they are not specifically identified as such: *"Praise Him, all His angels, praise Him, all His hosts!"*

Whereas cherubim are positioned beside and around the throne of God, the six-winged seraphim are seen as hovering above the throne as they minister in worship.

> *The Lord reigns; let the peoples tremble! He dwells between the cherubim; let the earth be moved!* (Psalm 99:1 NKJV)

> *The four living creatures, each having six wings, were full of eyes around and within. And they do not rest day or night, saying: "Holy, holy, holy, Lord God Almighty, Who was and is and is to come!"* (Revelation 4:8 NKJV)

**The Cherubim.** Cherubim are the created beings assigned to guard the throne of God as well as the ark of the covenant and the mercy seat.

> *And there I will meet with you, and I will speak with you from above the mercy seat, from between the two cherubim which are on the ark of the Testimony, about everything which I will give you in commandment to the children of Israel* (Exodus 25:22 NKJV).

> *The cherubim spread out their wings above, and covered the mercy seat with their wings. They faced one another; the faces of the cherubim were toward the mercy seat* (Exodus 37:9 NKJV).

Cherubim (plural for *cherub*) guarded the Tree of Life to keep man from eating of it and, therefore, living forever in his sins. Thus, contrary to popular belief, more than one angel guarded the entrance to Eden. The fullest description of cherubim is in Ezekiel 10 where they are closely related to the glory of God and have a part in the glory's presence and its withdrawal, moving at the Almighty's direction.[3]

*Then I looked, and, behold, in the firmament that was above the head of the cherubims there appeared over them as it were a sapphire stone, as the appearance of the likeness of a throne.*

*And He spake unto the man clothed with linen, and said, Go in between the wheels, even under the cherub, and fill thine hand with coals of fire from between the cherubims, and scatter them over the city. And he went in in my sight.*

*Now the cherubims stood on the right side of the house, when the man went in; and the cloud filled the inner court.*

*Then the glory of the Lord went up from the cherub, and stood over the threshold of the house; and the house was filled with the cloud, and the court was full of the brightness of the Lord's glory.*

*And the sound of the cherubims' wings was heard even to the outer court, as the voice of the Almighty God when He speaketh.*

*And it came to pass, that when He had commanded the man clothed with linen, saying, Take fire from between the wheels, from between the cherubims; then he went in, and stood beside the wheels.*

*And one cherub stretched forth his hand from between the cherubims unto the fire that was between the cherubims, and took thereof, and put it into the hands of him that was clothed with linen: who took it, and went out.*

*And there appeared in the cherubims the form of a man's hand under their wings.*

*And when I looked, behold the four wheels by the cherubims, one wheel by one cherub, and another wheel by another cherub: and the appearance of the wheels was as the colour of a beryl stone.*

*And as for their appearances, they four had one likeness, as if a wheel had been in the midst of a wheel.*

*When they went, they went upon their four sides; they turned not as they went, but to the place whither the head looked they followed it; they turned not as they went.*

*And their whole body, and their backs, and their hands, and their wings, and the wheels, were full of eyes round about, even the wheels that they four had.*

*As for the wheels, it was cried unto them in my hearing, O wheel.*

*And every one had four faces: the first face was the face of a cherub, and the second face was the face of a man, and the third the face of a lion, and the fourth the face of an eagle.*

*And the cherubims were lifted up. This is the living creature that I saw by the river of Chebar.*

*And when the cherubims went, the wheels went by them: and when the cherubims lifted up their wings to mount up from the earth, the same wheels also turned not from beside them.*

*When they stood, these stood; and when they were lifted up, these lifted up themselves also: for the spirit of the living creature was in them.*

*Then the glory of the Lord departed from off the threshold of the house, and stood over the cherubims.*

*And the cherubims lifted up their wings, and mounted up from the earth in my sight: when they went out, the wheels also were beside them, and every one stood at the door of the east gate of the Lord's house; and the glory of the God of Israel was over them above.*

*This is the living creature that I saw under the God of Israel by the river of Chebar; and I knew that they were the cherubims.*

*Every one had four faces apiece, and every one four wings; and the likeness of the hands of a man was under their wings.*

*And the likeness of their faces was the same faces which I saw by the river of Chebar, their appearances and themselves: they went every one straight forward* (Ezekiel 10:1-22 KJV).

Some of these angelic titles such as angels, archangels, seraphim, and cherubim are expounded on; others are not. Much of our understanding, then, is speculative. Still, some information we have on the angelic realm could be divine revelation through the Holy Spirit. We must learn as much as possible so as not to be deceived. And yet we don't want to get off in angelic worship of any kind or to any degree. We must always check our motives and the intents of our hearts. We must stay in balance and remember God is to be sought after, not heavenly beings. I always ask myself this question. "Who is first and foremost on my mind?" It must be the Father God, Jesus, and the Holy Spirit. They are not going to take a back seat to anyone, especially not one of their own servants!

Yet it is to be understood that angels are a structured society with different levels of authority, according to God's creative order (see Col. 1:16). Dr. Oral Roberts's theory on archangels is the simplest and the easiest for me to understand. He says:

> When God established the order of angels to worship Him and minister to people, He created three mighty archangels to rule over them: lucifer was a covering over God's throne, had power over the riches of the earth, was the most beautiful of all, and ruled over one-third of the angels. Gabriel seems to be the great military angel and makes the most important announcements from Heaven. Michael appears to be attached to Israel and in direct conflict with lucifer, who sinned against God and was cast down to the earth, along with one-third of the angels who followed him in rebellion. Lucifer became the devil, or satan, the archenemy of Christ and God's people.[4]

Even though there is no clear Scripture that names these three angels as archangels (except for Michael), it does seem to be logical since they are the only three angels mentioned by name.

In his book titled *Angels*, Billy Graham lists what he believes is an order of the angelic heavenly beings. They are archangels, angels, seraphim, cherubim, principalities, authorities, powers, thrones, might, and dominion. He points out that there are definite differences in the angels, even if it is not clearly spelled out in the Scripture as to what those differences are.[5]

Marilyn Hickey is one of the most balanced teachers of God's Word I have ever heard. In her book *Angels All Around*, she uses other "words" from the Scriptures to help define and place the angels in some type of performance order. She says, "Those angels who did not rebel with satan are called 'elect' angels":

> *I charge thee before God, and the Lord Jesus Christ, and the elect angels, that thou observe these things without preferring one before another, doing nothing by partiality* (I Timothy 5:21 KJV).

Marilyn also discusses the positions of "seraphim, cherubim, archangel, and guardian angels."[6]

These three respected ministers offer a congruent vein of thinking with regard to angelic rank and order according to God's Word. Based on my studies, I also agree that there is a definite military-type of structure among the angelic and demonic realm.

My encounters with the angels have not revealed any definition of authority, rank, or order. It has been interesting to note their military-type organization and stances, and it has been made clear to me by their visitations that certain groups are assigned specific tasks. For instance, the guardian angels assigned to individuals are a fairly clear example of human protection and direction through-out one's life, even from conception. (This was verified when I saw Malachi Charles' angel escort him to Heaven.)

Another story from Scripture that shows that some angels act as messengers sent on special assignments (like the military structure) is recorded in Judges 6:11-21 NKJV:

> *Now the Angel of the Lord came and sat under the terebinth tree which was in Ophrah, which belonged to Joash the Abiezrite,*

*while his son Gideon threshed wheat in the winepress, in order to hide it from the Midianites.*

*And the Angel of the Lord appeared to him, and said to him, "The Lord is with you, you mighty man of valor!"*

*Gideon said to Him, "O my lord, if the Lord is with us, why then has all this happened to us? And where are all His miracles which our fathers told us about, saying, 'Did not the Lord bring us up from Egypt?' But now the Lord has forsaken us and delivered us into the hands of the Midianites."*

*Then the Lord turned to him and said, "Go in this might of yours, and you shall save Israel from the hand of the Midianites. Have I not sent you?"*

*So he said to Him, "O my Lord, how can I save Israel? Indeed my clan is the weakest in Manasseh, and I am the least in my father's house."*

*And the Lord said to him, "Surely I will be with you, and you shall defeat the Midianites as one man."*

*Then he said to Him, "If now I have found favor in Your sight, then show me a sign that it is You who talk with me.*

*"Do not depart from here, I pray, until I come to You and bring out my offering and set it before You." And He said, "I will wait until you come back."*

*So Gideon went in and prepared a young goat, and unleavened bread from an ephah of flour. The meat he put in a basket, and he put the broth in a pot; and he brought them out to Him under the terebinth tree and presented them.*

*The Angel of God said to him, "Take the meat and the unleavened bread and lay them on this rock, and pour out the broth." And he did so.*

*Then the Angel of the Lord put out the end of the staff that was in His hand, and touched the meat and the unleavened bread; and fire rose out of the rock and consumed the meat and the unleavened bread. And the Angel of the Lord departed out of his sight.* (Judges 6:11-21 NKJV).

This passage of Scripture depicts that angels are faithful to carry out God's instructions quickly, perfectly, and obediently. The story even begins with a military tone as the angel calls Gideon "a mighty man of valor!" Then the angel gave him direction as to what he was to do. Gideon was not convinced, because he did not have the necessary personnel or equipment to complete the mission. The angel told him to follow the directions from the throne, and he would not fail.

When Gideon asked for a sign, the angel touched Gideon's offering with His staff, and fire rose out of the rock, consuming the sacrifice. The angel's actions and message ministered faith and courage to Gideon so that later he was able to overcome his fear and stand against Israel's enemies.

In this particular passage of Scripture this referenced Angel of the Lord could be Jesus, the Son of God, intervening between God and Man. Whether God sends an angel with a message, or whether it is the angel that has been assigned to you from conception with a message, or whether it is the Holy Spirit or Jesus directing and guiding our lives, seems quite irrelevant to me. How the angels are ranked and the order in which they operate is also

THE PRESENCE OF ANGELS IN YOUR LIFE

really unimportant. The important thing is that *there is divine protection, direction, and guidance* sent from the Father God to take care of His children.

## ENDNOTES

1. Jack W. Hayford, exec. ed., *Spirit-Filled Life Bible* (Nashville: Thomas Nelson, 1991), Word Wealth, 1409.

2. Ibid., Kingdom, 1945.

3. Ibid., Kingdom, 11.

4. Oral Roberts, *All You Ever Wanted to Know About Angels* (Tulsa, OK: Oral Roberts Evangelistic Association, 1994).

5. Billy Graham, *Angels* (Nashville: Thomas Nelson, 1995).

6. Marilyn Hickey, *Angels All Around* (Englewood, CO: Marilyn Hickey Ministries, 1992).

# 26

# DEMONS ARE REVEALED, TOO!

I have to admit that I want to see the angels, but I'm not sure I really want to see the demons, too. Trying to understand the physical description of demons may be too much for you as well, but just think of how Hollywood depicts the supernatural realm in the movies. Cheryl admits that some of what Hollywood portrays is very close to what she could describe as having seen of the demonic realm. I know the demonic realm is real, and I don't need to see it in a movie. I have seen demonic activity manifested and heard demons speak through people at numerous meetings over the years. Believe me, it isn't entertainment.

The danger is that Hollywood is desensitizing people to the spiritual realm and making a mockery out of anything having to do with God. I believe many in the motion picture, television, and music industries have stepped over the line and are actually dabbling in the demonic realm (through drug-induced hallucinations, promoting idol worship, and even portraying and demonstrating in their media various forms of demonic, ungodly activities). Satan uses Hollywood to show how powerful his forces are—spreading lies of fear and hopelessness with nothing to counteract them. But we know the truth. As you read this chapter, remember First John 4:4, *"...Greater is He that is in you, than he that is in the world"* (KJV).

— *Harry Salem II*

Since the angels have been revealed to me these last few years, the supernatural realm has become a part of my everyday life like never before. It seems everyone with whom I share my experiences says the same thing: "I wish I could see the angels." We must realize the supernatural realm is a parallel realm to this natural realm. There is definitely the good force of our Father God and His angels in the supernatural realm. However, there are also the devil and his demons to be reckoned with in the supernatural realm.

When God opened my spiritual eyes to see into the supernatural/parallel dimension, I saw both the good and the bad. I don't think most people who desire to see the angels want to see the demons as well. Yet, they all come together. It's like biting into a candy bar filled with caramel, peanuts, and chocolate and saying that you want to taste the caramel and chocolate but not the peanuts! It just doesn't work that way. You are about to get a mouthful of peanuts, like it or not! There's an old saying, "You get the water with the wet." Some things can't be separated.

Throughout the Bible we see angels in many different settings and manifested in different forms. Remember the story in Second Kings 6:15-17 that I mentioned in Chapter 1 about the prophet Elisha and his servant? The angels were present, surrounding the enemy. However, the angels were not seen by the servant until Elisha asked God to open the servant's eyes so he could see the multitudes surrounding them. What causes some to see angels while others do not? I don't know. There is no biblical teaching on this.

I do know that we must not get into condemnation because we can't see the angelic realm. Nor should we ever become puffed up or full of pride over our ability to see into the heavenly sphere if God allows it. Seeing angels really has no bearing on anything eternal. It does not change whether they exist or not. It doesn't change their abilities to do their God-given tasks. Nothing hinges on whether we see or not—but many things rest upon whether we believe or not.

Our ability to *believe* in the existence of God and His entire Kingdom is the foundation for dealing with and surviving in the spirit realm. Our belief even in the "unseen truths" of God's Word sets the pace and tone of our futures. We must never be carried away with every wind of doctrine but be biblically based in the sound doctrine of God's divine Word.

> *So then, we may no longer be children, tossed [like ships] to and fro between chance gusts of teaching and wavering with every changing wind of doctrine, [the prey of] the cunning and cleverness of unscrupulous men, [gamblers engaged] in every shifting form of trickery in inventing errors to mislead* (Ephesians 4:14).

When we know our position in Christ and we walk in His Word, we never have to be afraid of the demonic activity that is taking place upon the earth. But as warriors we need to be prepared for the onslaught, or attack, of the devil and his cohorts. Sometimes the demons can be a strong enemy, *but they are never stronger* than God and His angels. Don't be afraid. Be strong!

Many times when I am praying for people, God will open my spiritual eyes to the supernatural realm, and I will see manifestations of small, horrible-looking creatures (demons) that have attached themselves to God's people. These demons may be around their necks or on their backs or squeezing their heads. Does that mean they are possessed? Hardly! However, it does mean there could be uncrucified areas of their thought lives or of their flesh where there is still darkness. Satan will take advantage of any areas in our lives that are not surrendered to Christ.

Many times people are oppressed by the demonic enemy from generations before in areas that have been passed on to them from their ancestors—some of whom may not have served God.

> *You shall not bow down yourself to them or serve them; for I the Lord your God am a jealous God, visiting the iniquity of the fathers upon the children to the third and fourth generation of those who hate Me* (Exodus 20:5).

Since satan has dominion in darkness, he can come and harass people (even God's people) in those areas of darkness in their lives.

Demonic oppression can lead to or exacerbate suicide, anorexia, bulimia, overeating, etc. In working with people who are battling these problems, in the spiritual realm I have seen small, cowardly looking creatures that have long tendrils (rootlike extensions) that drip with slime. They usually have their victims wrapped up with many armlike extensions that have clawlike hands reaching into their minds and bodies.

Some of these demons even have a distinct odor that I can usually smell before I can see them. They really stink! They seem to be associated with people who are struggling with addiction and perversion. These demons are more fierce-looking in their faces than the others. They try to intimidate their victims and keep them in bondage by lying to them.

All of these demons seem to talk and whisper to their victims. They continuously try to convince their victim that he or she is unworthy, no good, a nobody. Remember, satan is the author of lies. He and all of his demonic buddies are master liars. Don't believe a word that they say. Jesus wouldn't listen to the lies when He was being tempted, and you must not either!

Every demonic spirit that I have seen is ugly. I mean really ugly! Can you imagine how ugly they have become? They have been cut off from the source of their beauty for thousands of years. No light from the Father God—only darkness, sin, and the devil.

All of these foul spirits are usually small in stature, extremely deformed, with filth, grime, slime, warts, tumors, and sores exuding from their horrible little forms. They don't have the form of man. They do have a type of body—a trunk, head, some semblance of legs, and arms that are root-like tendrils.

Every demonic creature I have seen has tormented-looking eyes (sometimes two eyes—sometimes many), drooling mouths, and the most horrible odor! They are not a pretty sight, but they are nothing to be afraid of, either. They are pathetic creatures who have no hope of ever being any different because of the choice they made to follow lucifer instead of staying in God's presence and remaining one of God's faithful angels.

I know that what I've shared with you may be hard to digest. Yet I can only be obedient in telling you what the Lord has allowed me to see. If I only told you about the angels, I would not be telling you all that I have seen. I do want you to understand that demons are just as real as the angels. However, they have no power over us except what we give them. Therefore, there is no need to fear.

# 27

# CAN ANGELS HURT YOU?

Here is some more great teaching from Cheryl's study on angels. God has promised us blessings and blessings. All He asks in return is our obedience.

— *Harry Salem II*

As I said in the last chapter, we don't have to be afraid of demons. But there are also certain angels who work for the Father God whose job it is to carry out the missions of calamity and woe. We don't have to be afraid of these angels, either. These angels are called "angels of destruction" in Psalm 78:49, *"He cast on them the fierceness of His anger, wrath, indignation, and trouble, by sending angels of destruction among them"* (NKJV).

Whether these angels are fallen angels or God's angels of service is discussed in almost every book on angels that I have read. It seems some believe one way while others believe the other.

Some believe that God is in control of these wicked forces and even uses them for His purposes. He used them to chasten His people, the Israelites, in Psalm 78:49.[1]

I tend to believe from my studies of God's Word that these angels are not demons. My opinion is that these are legitimate working angels who work for the Father and do His bidding when people choose to disobey God's commands. The Word says:

> And God sent an angel to Jerusalem to destroy it. As he was destroying, the Lord looked and relented of the disaster, and said to the angel who was destroying, "It is enough; now restrain your hand." And the angel of the Lord stood by the threshing floor...
> (I Chronicles 21:15 NKJV).

This passage doesn't call the angel "a destroying angel," but rather "an angel to destroy," and then also refers to this angel who was used to destroy as an "angel of the Lord." These phrases help me to form my opinion that these angels are not demons or fallen angels.

You may be thinking, *Yes, but that's all in the Old Testament—before the forgiveness of sins through the blood of Jesus.*

That's true, but we see an angel sent for destruction in Acts 12:23. This Scripture says, *"Then immediately an angel of the Lord struck him, because he did not give glory to God. And he was eaten by worms and died"* (NKJV). Taking God's glory and praise cost Herod his life. What a horrible death! And this destruction was carried out by "an angel of the Lord."

In another story in Acts, Ananias and Sapphira didn't fare too well, either. Their little rendezvous with death was after the death and resurrection of Jesus. Ananias and Sapphira sold a possession and secretly kept back part of the proceeds, taking the rest to Peter as if it were the whole amount. Ananias and Sapphira were judged for their hypocrisy and lying to God, not for their decision to retain some of their personal property for themselves.[2] When they lied to the apostles and stole God's money, they fell dead!

*But a certain man named Ananias, with Sapphira his wife, sold a possession. And he kept back part of the proceeds, his wife also being aware of it, and brought a certain part and laid it at the apostles' feet. But Peter said, "Ananias, why has Satan filled your heart to lie to the Holy Spirit and keep back part of the price of the land for yourself? While it remained, was it not your own? And after it was sold, was it not in your own control? Why have you conceived this thing in your heart? You have not lied to men but to God."*

*Then Ananias, hearing these words, fell down and breathed his last. So great fear came upon all those who heard these things. And the young men arose and wrapped him up, carried him out, and buried him.*

*Now it was about three hours later when his wife came in, not knowing what had happened. And Peter answered her, "Tell me whether you sold the land for so much?" She said, "Yes, for so much."*

*Then Peter said to her, "How is it that you have agreed together to test the Spirit of the Lord? Look, the feet of those who have buried your husband are at the door, and they will carry you out." Then immediately she fell down at his feet and breathed her last. And the young men came in and found her dead, and carrying her out, buried her by her husband. So great fear came upon all the church and upon all who heard these things (Acts 5:1-11 NKJV).*

Angels do what the Father tells them to do. They take their instructions from the Father God, and they are not inhibited by the things that limit humans: time, lack of knowledge, and lack of energy.[3]

> *Bless the Lord, you His angels, who excel in strength, who do His word, heeding the voice of His word* (Psalm 103:20 NKJV).

We can see from the above discussion that continual disobedience brings upon the wrath of the Father—the Father's judgment is carried out by His agents of destruction. Whether destruction comes on the earth or in the hereafter, continual disobedient sin brings destruction and judgment.

Remember, with God it is not always the action but it is the motive of the heart that determines His judgment (e.g., Ananias and Sapphira). God is just, fair, and I know that He loves us, His children. But just like any good earthly parent, God cannot ignore blatant disobedient behavior, or it will only get worse and possibly affect more than just the one who has chosen to be disobedient. God is good. God is just. God is fair. And sometimes that results in judgment.

Yes, angels can hurt you. They can and will hurt people who are in disobedience to God if the Father instructs them to do so. God's mercies endure forever, yet when is disobedience too much or too long? When do we cross that line of grace? How long can people sin and get away with it? I don't know, but I do know that we don't have to worry if we are choosing to walk in obedience to the Father God. I exhort you today, don't toy with walking the line of grace—God's Word says that every disobedience receives a just reward.

*For if the word spoken through angels proved steadfast, and every transgression and disobedience received a just reward, how shall we escape if we neglect so great a salvation...?* (Hebrews 2:2-3 NKJV)

Instead, choose to obey and be blessed. It is not worth it to play with sin and disobedience. It is so simple to follow God's law, obey Him, and receive His wonderful rewards. Sin brings destruction and judgment. Righteousness brings all of God: His blessings, His rewards, all that is wonderful!

## ENDNOTES

1. Lester Sumrall, *Angels: The Messengers of God* (South Bend, IN: LeSea Pub., 1993), 24.

2. Jack W. Hayford, exec. ed., *Spirit-Filled Life Bible* (Nashville: Thomas Nelson, 1991), Commentary, 1633.

3. Sumrall, 36.

# 28

## ANGELIC ESCORTS

Our boys have a faith that is unshakable and their prayers get answers, as you'll read here. Cheryl got a surprising confirmation on a visit to her mother's home. I reminded Cheryl that if you believe more in what you see in the supernatural than what you see in the natural, then you will have it. She got what she and the boys were believing for.

— *Harry Salem II*

What a glorious thought and assurance that the angel who has been with me from the womb will escort me to my heavenly home and into the arms of my Savior, Jesus! Since seeing Malachi Charles (the baby we miscarried) being escorted to Heaven, I believe the angels can and will help us cross over to Heaven when we go home.

When my earthly daddy died, I assume he must have had the most glorious experience! It was a beautiful spring day. My mother was in the garden planting, and Daddy was trying to help her. Although Daddy had experienced multiple strokes and his health had been deteriorating for 11 years, he still wanted to be right by Mama's side. This day was no different. Mother was doing the planting, and Daddy was enjoying the sunshine and "directing" the gardening project. About halfway through the morning, Daddy told Mama that he wasn't feeling his best. Mother told him to go and sit on the porch and rest while she finished the planting.

She watched him cross the road and climb the steps of the porch. Then Daddy sat down in his chair on the porch. As Mama leaned back down to continue covering the seeds, she heard a sound like a yell or a scream. She looked up to see what was the matter.

As she did, she saw Daddy sitting on the porch with his arms straight up in the air, and his eyes open wide with surprise. His mouth was also shaped in a position of surprise. When Mama ran across the road to Daddy, she couldn't get his arms down or change the expression on his face. Daddy had gone to be with Jesus. I believe he saw the angels and threw his arms up to greet them—and maybe even to say to Mama that he had to go!

This may not seem like much to you, but this has been a great comfort to me. You see, my daddy is the one who taught me to study God's Word, to seek for the spirit realm beyond what we can see, and to dream big dreams.

When Mother related to me Daddy's crossing over, I felt the expression he left behind was a word to us to expect the angel's coming. Could it be that Daddy was leaving us a message that this trip to Heaven is exciting, fascinating, and wonderful? I believe so.

Luke 16:22 says, *"So it was that the beggar died, and was carried by the angels to Abraham's bosom..."* (NKJV). I believe that when Daddy died he was gloriously escorted to meet His Lord and Savior by his guardian angel who had been assigned to him since before he was born.

It was very difficult for Mama. She missed him terribly. Because of this, our two sons, Harry and Roman, prayed for her every night since "Gran Gran" (my daddy) went to Heaven. They always prayed the same prayer over her—for the angels to watch over her, to keep her safe, and to help her not feel lonely. I believe the Holy Spirit and God's angels did just that!

One weekend not too long after Daddy died, we were visiting Mama, and everyone was outside except for me. I was in the kitchen preparing supper. Usually my mother is doing this because she is a "doer," and she shows her love by "doing" for everyone. But this time she was outside watching the children, and I was alone at the kitchen sink.

All of a sudden I felt an angelic presence, and I turned around. Standing in the doorway was an angel, not saying a word but definitely watching over everything. I said, "So, you are the one assigned to her." Nothing was said audibly, but the greatest peace fell over the house. I believe that I saw my mother's guardian angel.

All the fears and frustrations seemed to vanish with the comfort of knowing that my mom is looked after, watched over, and cared for by the messenger sent by God. I really couldn't watch over her anyway, but God can and He does.

God will utilize whatever is necessary to accomplish His mission on the earth. I don't know why my dad had to die when he did, but I have total assurance that God is protecting my mom and watching over her through the angel that I met that day in the kitchen in Choctaw County, Mississippi.

A few years later, my mama remarried. A wonderful and precious, godly man, Grandpa James (McAdams) was a most precious gift from God to my mama. They were married for almost 12 years before he crossed over to Heaven. My mama is once again physically alone, but never truly alone, for I know she has a big angel with her at all times, plus the promise from Heaven that, *"...I will never leave you nor forsake you"* (Heb. 13:5 NKJV).

## 29

# ANGELS CAME FOR HER... I SAID, "NOT YET."

When our precious daughter, Gabrielle Christian, was born on May 26, 1993, I held her in my arms and I knew she was going to break my heart. In fact, I whispered those words in her tiny little ears. As she grew each day, I loved her more and more. I teased with everyone that the day she was born I bought a dog and a gun, because I knew there would never be a man good enough to marry my daughter. It was a huge thing inside this Daddy's heart to imagine having to walk Gabrielle down the aisle someday and "hand her over" to another man. The day she crossed over to Heaven, I realized the only man perfect enough for me to give her to is Jesus. That day, I walked her as far as I could go, and then Jesus took her hand for the rest of the journey.

— *Harry Salem II*

After our 6-year-old daughter, Gabrielle, had struggled with an inoperable brain tumor for 11 months, it came down to one angelic night. It had been an extremely hard week. We had fought death back from our door day and night for months, and this particular week had been a fight for life, minute by minute. But despite how much we believed, how many prayers we prayed, how hard we fought, we were losing ground. It was obvious to everyone, except maybe us. We had been in this fight so long that we only knew how to fight…that's all—fight. We stood, we believed.

People, friends, family, it seemed like everyone was converging on our home all at the same time over the weekend before Thanksgiving. Person after person came and went; we hardly noticed. We did not have time for pleasantries, or hospitality. We were in a fight against death! We had on every piece of armor, every bit of battle-weary fatigue had begun to set in on us, but we never lowered our shield of faith or our sword of the Spirit. But the fight was relentless. I was sick, literally sick in my physical body, but I didn't have time for sick. I was pushing, Harry was pushing, Tracey and the boys were pushing. It's all we knew to do and we did it with our heads held high, and never once did we let our faith slide. Not once! But still the end came.

One of our fathers in faith came to our home to try and talk us off the wall, at least that was the way it seemed to me. I saw our family operating as Nehemiah did—obeying God and building the wall to protect God's people while others came to tell him to stop building. Our spiritual father told us to let her go, that this fight was going to kill more than Gabrielle if we didn't let up.

I was angry; furious may be an even better word! I lashed out on the inside with every bit of strength I could muster. I thought, *How can we continue to fight the enemy of death when even family, friends, and spiritual fathers come into our home and say they have given up?* But that is not what I said. I said, "That's easy for you to say, 'Let her go.' You are an old man and lived a long life. You are ready to cross over to eternity. She is six years old and has not had her opportunity to live her life here. No! I won't let her go. I won't!" With that, I stomped out of the room, furious, agitated, and very cross with everyone. *We don't need this,* I thought to myself.

But after a few more days of watching her slip away, further and further from the earth, I was beginning to see what others had already seen. I didn't want to see it. I didn't want to accept it, but still, there it was...staring back at Harry and me as we watched life slip right out of her, no matter how hard we held on. And we held on; that's for sure. You may have heard of a "death grip" before. But until you saw the way we held Gabrielle on the earth with our sheer will and faith you have not seen a "death grip."

It was Sunday afternoon, and the Holy Spirit was reminding me of another afternoon, months earlier in July, when Gabrielle had almost left the earth during this long and drawn-out fight for life. Once that battle was won, we all took communion together, and Gabrielle and I had made a commitment to one another that we would not leave the other one behind on this earth. I had no intention of leaving her behind, but she was a little girl and Heaven was not so far from her entry here on earth. After all, she had only been here 6 years. The smell of Heaven was still on her. I wanted her to make a commitment to me, to her daddy, to her family, that she would stand and fight, not give up, and win this battle until it was finished. She made the pact with me. I could sleep a few hours again after that.

But here we were again, months later, and the Holy Spirit reminded me of that covenant she had made with me. He urged me to bring it up and talk with her about it. I know you must be thinking, *Gabrielle was only 6 years old. What could she understand about such things?* I know, I know, but she did understand. She had understanding and wisdom way beyond her years. I knew we had to talk. I knew that I was not yielding at all to the Holy Spirit's prompting. I knew that I was being stubborn, strong-willed in my faith, and I was not yielding to Him or being soft to His presence. I had dug in and it would take Heaven to move me from my spot.

I sat beside our daughter on the bed. She had fought hard for 11 months and she was barely able to breathe. I had already started giving her morphine for the pain, but she was conscious, and she understood when I talked even though she was long past communicating with words to anyone. I asked her if she remembered the communion we had taken together and our commitment to each other. She squeezed my hand. I told her that I trusted her to make the right choice and to listen to the Father God. She squeezed my hand again. She knew what she was doing.

I talked some more with her, and with my heart breaking inside, I promised her that I would stand and fight without hesitation until this war was over and she was completely well again if that was what she wanted. I asked her if she understood. She squeezed my hand again.

I didn't want to ask her this, but I knew I must. I asked her if she wanted to stay here or if she wanted to go to be with Jesus. I told her Mommy would be fine, no matter what she chose. I told her if she went on to Heaven, that I would not be far behind and I would be alright left here for a little while. Then, as I held the sweet hands of Harry's and my precious daughter, I asked the question that I needed her to answer. "Do you want to go and be with Jesus?" She squeezed my hand. Inside I was devastated, but I knew she had made her choice and I had to let her go. I had released Gabrielle from our covenant.

From that Sunday afternoon until Tuesday morning at 6:55 A.M. I never left her side. I never closed my eyes. She was slipping away and I couldn't bear it, but I was not going to miss it, either. Every moment was one I would cherish until we were together again. I was strong. Harry was strong. He never left, either. Sometimes he tried to catnap, but only a few minutes at a time. Neither of us was ready. Monday came and went; Monday night came upon us. I was sitting in my chair beside the bed in which she lay. Harry was lying beside her. Her eyes were open most of the time. She had long passed being able to smile, but inside that precious body I knew she was smiling. She always smiled.

Sometime during the night I felt them coming. I looked up and there they were—the angels were coming down the hallway. I knew they were coming for her. I immediately held out my hand in a "STOP" motion, and I said, "Not yet." They obeyed. They quietly backed down the hallway, but they didn't turn around, only backed out still facing us. A few hours later they came again, taking the same path, down the hall. I held out my hand for them to stop and I said, "Not yet, I'm not ready." A few hours later they came again, and still I would not let them come too close. They were so patient and precious, never pushing. They backed out the door and down the hallway again the third time.

At 6:55 A.M., I felt an uncontrollable sleep coming upon me. I had drunk enough coffee to stay awake for ten years—there was no way this was happening! But it was—sleep was coming on me like I had an IV in my arm and was being put under by anesthesia! I quickly tapped Harry and said that I had to lay my head down for "just five minutes." Even as I was saying the words I was slipping into unconsciousness.

Harry said it was only five minutes before she was crossing over. He said as my head was laying down beside her little precious body, she began blowing kisses, which was a miracle as she had lost her ability to move her lips in that way. He felt she was blowing kisses at him as if to say, "Daddy, I'll see you later!" It was only minutes, before he knew she was almost gone. Harry sat beside her, and with my head laying on her other side, she slipped away into eternity. Harry softly said, "There she goes," and before he could even finish the sentence, he audibly heard the voice of the Father God say, "Here she comes!"

How close this earth realm is to eternity! How quickly we can pass through the portal we call death—but what it truly is, is the birthing canal from the womb of earth into real life—life eternal! All of Heaven waits to rejoice as we cross over to really live! Real life is not here. The angels live in the real realm of life. We await our appointed time, in the womb of life, "mother earth," so to speak.

In these last days as there are numerous and various earthquakes as the Bible predicts there will be, I can't help but think that the earth is in labor and soon we will all be going home to real life, to really live! Angels await our homecoming, of this I am certain. I have total assurance that our precious and most precocious daughter Gabrielle is now with the angels and many of our loved ones who have gone on before us. I can just imagine her making preparations along with Jesus for our soon arrival...but all in His time, not ours. We await instructions from His throne. Our lives are not our own, we are under command of the most high God!

# 30

# FULL CIRCLE

September 11, 2001. If all had gone according to plan, that morning we would have been in Battery Park, shooting video footage for a television show. We ended up delaying the trip into the city, and now we know why. God truly does order our steps.

— *Harry Salem II*

During September 11, 2001, we were in New York when the terrorists hit the twin towers. We were not able to fly out as there were no flights going anywhere, so we did what we do best. We prayed. As we always do, we asked the Lord to order our steps and boy did He ever!

We left New York City and drove to Syracuse, New York, to preach Friday night through Sunday morning services for Pastor John and Lisa Carter. What an amazing outpouring of God's mercy and grace we had in those services. We had known for quite some time that the anointing for God's restoration was upon our family ministry, so we were not surprised when we found ourselves in and among millions of people in this part of the country, on this very date in history, searching for answers and desperately needing God's healing touch of restoration. After Sunday morning services, we drove to Buffalo, New York for Sunday evening service with Pastor Tommy and Wanda Reid.

This was almost like we had come full circle, as this was the very church where I had begun to see the angels in the beginning chapter of this book. As the worship began and then flowed deeper and deeper, further into the very depths of God's throne, I felt that same presence of angelic beings filling the sanctuary. I looked up to see an all-too-familiar sight. The ceiling was covered with hundreds, maybe thousands, of angels. It is so hard to estimate numbers when looking into the realm of the supernatural as we measure by our own dimension. The spiritual realm is so much more multidimensional than ours here on earth that well...let's just say legions of angels. That should suffice!

There they were in all the splendor that I had remembered from earlier visitations. They were huge really, so very tall and muscular. They were dressed with royal looking garments, multicolored with every hue of the rainbow, not just in the fabrics of their clothing, but even in the very essence of their beings. They were filled with light and all kinds of colors—too many colors to even try and identify honestly. The colors flowed as if they were in unison and yet they were completely individual. As each angel moved with quickness and yet pinpoint accuracy, the space that their "matter" had left dissipated with the same emanating color that they possessed.

I didn't hesitate this time to share with Harry, who was standing right beside me on the platform as we were getting ready to preach and minister that evening. I tugged on his sleeve and whispered in his ear, "Do you see them? Can you see them filling the ceiling with their beings?" I was so excited and Harry was too at this point because he knew by now that when I see the angels it is for a purpose; the Father God is showing me something, or teaching me something, that I am to share with others.

Harry answered me quickly that he could not see them, but he said he could feel their presence all around in the atmosphere. All of a sudden, as if under the command of the highest general, each angel put his hand on the butt end of his sword, and with precision beyond anything I can describe with human words, in complete unison, they pulled their swords from their sheaths. The sound was almost deafening. I wanted to cover my ears! Not only was it loud, but it was unnerving as well. Now, thousands upon thousands of angels stood at attention with swords drawn and lifted in the air in perfect military attack position.

My thoughts were racing; my heart was pounding. I was quite certain that in witnessing this event of the pulling of these swords, that we in the realm of the earth had just crossed a turning point, a defining moment, that would never be undone again this side of Heaven. As I searched my heart for the sound of His still small voice, I listened. I waited for an answer. Soon I felt the Holy Spirit whisper to me, "These swords will never return to their sheaths until after Jesus comes for His Bride and the devil is thrown into the bottomless pit."

So that was it; that was the line that had been drawn in the sand by the Father God. This was war, war like no other war. This was the end of time as we had ever known it. In the ten years since that meeting I have seen the angels many times in services around the country, but never have I seen those swords put away in their sheaths. Time is short for this side of Heaven. The line has been drawn and there is no turning back now. The enemy is defeated but we must learn to draw our own swords and keep them high and lifted up. We must never back down or turn around again, not as a country, a nation under God, a people, a family, a marriage, or an individual. We must hold up our swords of the Spirit, which is the Word of God, according to Ephesians 6, and know with whom we fight.

> *Therefore take up the whole armor of God, that you may be able to withstand in the evil day, and having done all, to stand. Stand therefore, having girded your waist with truth, having put on the breastplate of righteousness, and having shod your feet with the preparation of the gospel of peace; above all, taking the shield of faith with which you will be able to quench all the fiery darts of the wicked one. And take the helmet of salvation, and the sword of the Spirit, which is the word of God; praying always with all prayer and supplication in the Spirit, being watchful to this end with all perseverance and supplication for all the saints* (Ephesians 6:13-18 NKJV).

We must not be lax in drawing our weapons of warfare. Our weaponry is, literally, the Word of God. Our Bibles are our shields and they must be pulled from their sheaths each and every day if we plan on withstanding in the evil day. The evil day is upon us, yet a complacent attitude has come upon God's people like the poppy field outside the Emerald City in the *The Wizard of Oz* movie. This seems to be the most prevailing of atmospheres. Within God's people there is so much emphasis on surviving in a bad economy, ore money, having more possessions, and getting what *I* want, instead of knowing what *He* wants! We have become so self-centered that it is difficult even finding a group of people within the known Church of America that is completely sold out to His will. More self-absorbed than Holy Spirit led is what we have seen as we have traveled for these many years across this great country.

There is no way to get around particular Scriptures written to this generation of churchgoers, who call themselves the Bride of Christ.

> *Not everyone who says to Me, Lord, Lord, will enter the king-dom of heaven, but he who does the will of My Father Who is in heaven. Many will say to Me on that day, Lord, Lord, have we not prophesied in Your name and driven out demons in Your name and done many mighty works in Your name? And then I will say to them openly (publicly), I never knew you; depart from Me, you who act wickedly [disregarding My commands]* (Matthew 7:21-23).

The key to a right relationship with Jesus is not about pray-ing the right prayer at the right time. It is not about growing up in America, or even in church. It is about obeying the voice of the Father through the Holy Spirit and His Word. What He tells us we must do; it is not up for debate or discussion. Did Moses get to "talk God out of" His plan when Moses' own inadequacies or his inabilities were staring him in the face? I think not. We must learn to obey if we want to truly be called His own. For Jesus to eternally know us, our lives must be about Him, His will, His pur-pose—not our own. We must learn to obey Him, His voice, His still small voice when it goes with the grain of our thinking and even when it goes against the grain of what we want to do.

Obedience is not about what we want. It is all about being "dead to ourselves" and alive in Christ. His way is the only way to eternal life. When we can live our lives with the understanding that we don't own our lives—we freely gave our lives to Christ and we took His life and His way of life—then we can go through anything, any circumstance, any situation, and eventually arrive in victory—through Christ, not in any doing of our own.

# 31

## In Conclusion

I still haven't seen the angels, but I know someday I will. I hope after reading this book, you can agree with me that Cheryl has seen the angels and her descriptions and depictions of them are true and accurate. Most of all, I hope you believe that angels are real and appear as God allows, because they are here for us, not to be worshiped, but to help us. And, above all, be open to all that God has for you.

— *Harry Salem II*

I hope that you have been able to feel my heart in these pages. Hopefully you have been inspired, encouraged, and edified by this book. It has been my desire to answer many questions that you may have had concerning angels. But my greatest desire is to remind you that the angels are yet another one of God's benefits just for you. I pray that you feel more confident in your relationship with the Father God. I pray that you feel challenged to dedicate more of yourself to His service today than you did yesterday.

My hope, as I have shared some remarkable stories with you, is that your heart can feel and hear the sincerity of mine. My motives for writing this book are pure before God. I am humbled by God choosing to use me to write this book. Please, know my heart.

I am just a country girl from Choctaw County, Mississippi, but I guess if God could send an angel to find Hagar *"...by a spring of water in the wilderness on the road to Shur"* (Gen. 16:7), He could certainly send one to find me in the woods of Choctaw County.

The Father God knows where you are, too. He loves you so much and desires the very best for your life. You can count on it. I did.

I leave you with one last thought. There really are no words to describe how I feel about seeing the angels. But I know that if God had never allowed me to literally see them, I would still believe they are real.

If you are one of God's redeemed children, take heart in knowing that one day—you too *will* see the angels. So whether your eyes are opened to the supernatural realm while you are on this earth or if you behold them when you actually cross over into eternity, it is irrelevant. The angels are real, created by our Father God for our behalf—and the angels *will be revealed* to you.

Be encouraged that you will be blessed as you believe, even if you do not see. For Jesus Himself promises that blessing in John 20:29, *"Jesus said to him, 'Thomas, because you have seen Me, you have believed. Blessed are those who have not seen and yet have believed.'"* (NKJV).

# QUESTIONS & ANSWERS

**Did you know angels tell us *never* to worship them?**

Look at Revelation 22:8-9:

> *And I John saw these things, and heard them. And when I had heard and seen, I fell down to worship before the feet of the angel which shewed me these things. Then saith he unto me, See thou do it not: for I am thy fellowservant, and of thy brethren the prophets, and of them which keep the sayings of this book: worship God* (KJV).

The angels are God's messengers and ministering servants. That means they are not to be worshiped. God alone is worthy to receive glory and honor and power, for He created all things.

> *Thou art worthy, O Lord, to receive glory and honour and power: for Thou hast created all things, and for Thy pleasure they are and were created* (Revelation 4:11 KJV).

## Did you know that angels can go before you and help you succeed?

Genesis 24 tells a beautiful story about God sending an angel before Abraham's servant to help the servant find Isaac a wife.

*The Lord God of heaven, who took me from my father's house and from the land of my family, and who spoke to me and swore to me, saying, "To your descendants I give this land," He will send His angel before you, and you shall take a wife for my son from there* (Genesis 24:7 NKJV).

The angel goes before the servant and sets up the scenario. The servant meets Rebekah as she comes to the well and draws water for him and his camels.

*Now the young woman was very beautiful to behold, a virgin; no man had known her. And she went down to the well, filled her pitcher, and came up. And the servant ran to meet her and said, "Please let me drink a little water from your pitcher." So she said, "Drink, my lord." Then she quickly let her pitcher down to her hand, and gave him a drink. And when she had finished giving him a drink, she said, "I will draw water for your camels also, until they have finished drinking"* (Genesis 24:16-19 NKJV).

God confirms that this is to be Isaac's wife. How did the servant know which one to pick? Because God's angel had gone before him to make the way clear and plain.

## Did you know that angels are very intelligent?

God created angels with great wisdom to help Him in the earth, *"...according to the wisdom of the angel of God, to know everything that is in the earth"* (2 Sam. 14:20 NKJV).

How can they know the things they need to know on the earth? I believe they have close relationship with the Holy Spirit (like we do), who is omnipresent. He knows all and is at all places at all times. I believe the Holy Spirit shares with the angels what they need to know so they can successfully accomplish their missions.

## Did you know that we cannot hide from God or from His ministering angelic servants?

I tell my children that those things that are done or said in secret are not really secret at all. God truly is watching us through the Holy Spirit and through the angels. God has angels called "watchers" that are watching for God. Daniel 4:13 says, *"I saw in the visions of my head while on my bed, and there was a watcher, a holy one, coming down from heaven"* (NKJV).

Daniel 4:17 also makes reference to these angels:

*This decision is by the decree of the watchers, and the sentence by the word of the holy ones, in order that the living may know that the Most High rules in the kingdom of men...* (NKJV).

So, we are not alone no matter what we do or say. It is seen and heard! That can be a positive if your heart is clean before the Lord.

## Did you know that angels are the reapers of the harvest?

Matthew 13:39 says, *"The enemy who sowed them is the devil, the harvest is the end of the age, and the reapers are the angels"* (NKJV). Jesus is making reference that the angels are going to come and "reap" us out of this world in the Rapture. We are going to leave this place with a triumph procession, escorted by the angels. What a wonderful way to go!

## Did you know that the angels have their very own language?

This heavenly angelic language must be accessible to us as humans because Paul says in First Corinthians 13:1, *"Though I speak with the tongues of men and of angels..."* (KJV). Although some view the reference to the *"tongues of angels"* as a poetic hyperbole, it likely denotes the languages of these supernatural beings.[1] This says to me there is a distinct language that the angels speak that is different from man.

In this particular Scripture, Paul was trying to teach the relative importance of speaking in tongues, and also the times that it would be beneficial. It seems that he spoke in both the language of men (in his time it was Greek), and he spoke in the language of the angels (tongues). I know the angels can understand my earthly language, but I love it that I have access to the angelic language of tongues.

## Did you know that some angels will preach on the earth?

They do according to Revelation 14:6:

*And I saw another angel fly in the midst of heaven, having the everlasting gospel to preach unto them that dwell on the earth, and to every nation, and kindred, and tongue, and people* (KJV).

Wow! Preaching angels! I wonder if they'll use television, radio, or satellite—or if they will need to? How wonderful that an angel of God will preach the Gospel of truth, coming directly against the antichrist's system of unbelief and wickedness.[2]

## Did you know that angels are moved (or not moved) by our words, that is, prayers?

See for yourself in this Scripture, *"...Your words were heard, and I have come as a consequence of [and in response to] your words"* (Dan. 10:12).

Let's look at the same verse in the NIV: *"...Your words were heard, and I have come in response to them."* The angel told Daniel that he was dispatched from God's throne with the answer from the first time Daniel prayed.

Also the Scripture says in Acts 10:4:

*...And the angel said to him, Your prayers and your [generous] gifts to the poor have come up [as a sacrifice] to God and have been remembered by Him.*

God hears our prayers and enlists His angels to do work for Him.

Another Scripture that points out the importance of our words is when the angel was speaking to Zachariah in Luke 1:11-13:

*And there appeared to him an angel of the Lord, standing at the right side of the altar of incense. And when Zachariah saw him, he was troubled, and fear took possession of him. But the angel said to him, Do not be afraid, Zachariah, because your petition was heard, and your wife Elizabeth will bear you a son, and you must call his name John [God is favorable].*

The angel told Zachariah that God heard his heartfelt prayer to have a son. Our prayers are vitally important in keeping the angels moving in our behalf.

## Did you know that sometimes angels come to people in dreams?

They did to Joseph in Matthew 1:20:

*But while he thought on these things, behold, the angel of the Lord appeared unto him in a dream, saying, Joseph, thou son of David, fear not to take unto thee Mary thy wife: for that which is conceived in her is of the Holy Ghost* (KJV).

Sometimes we need answers and we are so confused that we cannot hear God's voice through the onslaught of voices that are raging in our minds.

I'm sure Joseph felt confused and had a thousand thoughts racing through his mind when he found out that Mary became pregnant while they were betrothed (engaged).

*Then Joseph her husband, being a just man, and not willing to make her a publick example, was minded to put her away privily* (Matthew 1:19 KJV).

I can relate to being confused and needing to hear from the Lord clearly. When I saw Gabion (my guardian angel) the first time, I was struggling with much inner turmoil. After I saw him, my fear of being alone in the battle was resolved. Obviously, Joseph received assurance from the angel's words because he took Mary as his wife.

*Then Joseph being raised from sleep did as the angel of the Lord had bidden him, and took unto him his wife: and knew her not till she had brought forth her firstborn son: and he called His name Jesus* (Matthew 1:24-25 KJV).

# Did you know that holy angels will attend Christ at His second coming?

The angels are going to be an intricate part of the grand finale of Christ's return. Matthew 25:31 says:

*When the Son of man shall come in His glory, and all the holy angels with Him, then shall He sit upon the throne of His glory* (KJV).

That would be a great day to be a holy angel!

There will be much angelic activity through spiritual warfare in the end times, according to the Book of Revelation in God's Word. The casting down of satan results from a great battle between the hosts of Heaven and the hordes of hell.

*And there was war in heaven: Michael and his angels fought against the dragon; and the dragon fought and his angels, and prevailed not; neither was their place found any more in heaven.*

*And the great dragon was cast out, that old serpent, called the Devil, and Satan, which deceiveth the whole world: he was cast out into the earth, and his angels were cast out with him.*

*And I heard a loud voice saying in heaven, Now is come salvation, and strength, and the kingdom of our God, and the power of His Christ: for the accuser of our brethren is cast down, which accused them before our God day and night.*

*And they overcame him by the blood of the Lamb, and by the word of their testimony; and they loved not their lives unto the death* (Revelation 12:7-11 KJV).

In this battle, Heaven's warriors force satan and his demons forever from the heavenly realm. But we must note that victory is not achieved solely by the angels, but also by believers' use of spiritual weapons. The angels fight, but God's saints provide the "fire power." This is clearly shown by Revelation 12:11, *"And they overcame him by the blood of the Lamb, and by the word of their testimony..."* (KJV). The angels did not overcome the accuser alone; the saints were in partnership through prayer-warfare. The angels were God's means for administering the victory, which prayer enforced.[3]

Yes, the King of kings and Lord of lords is coming.

*And He will send His angels with a great sound of a trumpet, and they will gather together His elect from the four winds, from one end of heaven to the other* (Matthew 24:31 NKJV).

*And* [He will] *give relief to you who are troubled, and to us as well. This will happen when the Lord Jesus is revealed from heaven in blazing fire with His powerful angels* (2 Thessalonians 1:7 NIV).

## ENDNOTES

1. Jack W. Hayford, exec. ed., *Spirit-Filled Life Bible* (Nashville: Thomas Nelson, 1991), Commentary, 1739.

2. Lester Sumrall, *Angels: The Messengers of God* (South Bend, IN: LeSea Publishing, 1993), 24.

3. *Spirit-Filled Life Bible*, Kingdom, 1977.

# SELECTED SCRIPTURE REFERENCES

## KING JAMES VERSION

### Phrase: WATCHER

*I saw in the visions of my head upon my bed, and, behold, a watcher and an holy one came down from heaven* (Daniel 4:13 KJV).

*And whereas the king saw a watcher and an holy one coming down from heaven, and saying, Hew the tree down, and destroy it; yet leave the stump of the roots thereof in the earth, even with a band of iron and brass, in the tender grass of the field; and let it be wet with the dew of heaven, and let his portion be with the beasts of the field, till seven times pass over him* (Daniel 4:23 KJV).

### Phrase: WATCHERS

*Make ye mention to the nations; behold, publish against Jerusa-lem, that watchers come from a far country, and give out their voice against the cities of Judah* (Jeremiah 4:16 KJV).

*This matter is by the decree of the watchers, and the demand by the word of the holy ones: to the intent that the living may know that the most High ruleth in the kingdom of men, and giveth it to whomsoever He will, and setteth up over it the basest of men* (Daniel 4:17 KJV).

## Phrase: PRINCIPALITIES

*Say unto the king and to the queen, Humble yourselves, sit down: for your principalities shall come down, even the crown of your glory* (Jeremiah 13:18 KJV).

*For I am persuaded, that neither death, nor life, nor angels, nor principalities, nor powers, nor things present, nor things to come... shall be able to separate us from the love of God...in Christ Jesus our Lord* (Romans 8:38-39 KJV).

*To the intent that now unto the principalities and powers in heavenly places might be known by the church the manifold wisdom of God* (Ephesians 3:10 KJV).

*For we wrestle not against flesh and blood, but against principalities, against powers, against the rulers of the darkness of this world, against spiritual wickedness in high places* (Ephesians 6:12 KJV).

*For by Him were all things created, that are in heaven, and that are in earth, visible and invisible, whether they be thrones, or dominions, or principalities, or powers: all things were created by Him, and for Him* (Colossians 1:16 KJV).

*And having spoiled principalities and powers, He made a shew of them openly, triumphing over them in it* (Colossians 2:15 KJV).

*Put them in mind to be subject to principalities and powers, to obey magistrates, to be ready to every good work* (Titus 3:1 KJV).

## Phrase: SONS OF GOD (Angels/Believers)

*That the sons of God saw the daughters of men that they were fair; and they took them wives of all which they chose* (Genesis 6:2 KJV).

*There were giants in the earth in those days; and also after that, when the sons of God came in unto the daughters of men, and they bare children to them, the same became mighty men which were of old, men of renown* (Genesis 6:4 KJV).

*Now there was a day when the sons of God came to present themselves before the Lord, and Satan came also among them* (Job 1:6 KJV).

*Again there was a day when the sons of God came to present themselves before the Lord, and Satan came also among them to present himself before the Lord* (Job 2:1 KJV).

*When the morning stars sang together, and all the sons of God shouted for joy?* (Job 38:7 KJV)

*Yet the number of the children of Israel shall be as the sand of the sea, which cannot be measured nor numbered; and it shall come to pass, that in the place where it was said unto them, Ye are not My people, there it shall be said unto them, Ye are the sons of the living God* (Hosea 1:10 KJV).

*But as many as received Him, to them gave He power to become the sons of God, even to them that believe on His name* (John 1:12 KJV).

*For as many as are led by the Spirit of God, they are the sons of God* (Romans 8:14 KJV).

*For the earnest expectation of the creature waiteth for the manifestation of the sons of God* (Romans 8:19 KJV).

*And because ye are sons, God hath sent forth the Spirit of His Son into your hearts, crying, Abba, Father* (Galatians 4:6 KJV).

*That ye may be blameless and harmless, the sons of God, without rebuke, in the midst of a crooked and perverse nation, among whom ye shine as lights in the world* (Philippians 2:15 KJV).

*Behold, what manner of love the Father hath bestowed upon us, that we should be called the sons of God: therefore the world knoweth us not, because it knew Him not* (I John 3:1 KJV).

*Beloved, now are we the sons of God, and it doth not yet appear what we shall be: but we know that, when He shall appear, we shall be like Him; for we shall see Him as He is* (I John 3:2 KJV).

## Phrase: HOST

*Thus the heavens and the earth were finished, and all the host of them* (Genesis 2:1 KJV).

*And when Jacob saw them, he said, This is God's host: and he called the name of that place Mahanaim* (Genesis 32:2 KJV).

*And lest thou lift up thine eyes unto heaven, and when thou seest the sun, and the moon, and the stars, even all the host of heaven, shouldest be driven to worship them, and serve them, which the Lord thy God hath divided unto all nations under the whole heaven* (Deuteronomy 4:19 KJV).

*And hath gone and served other gods, and worshipped them, either the sun, or moon, or any of the host of heaven, which I have not commanded* (Deuteronomy 17:3 KJV).

*And he said, Nay; but as captain of the host of the Lord am I now come. And Joshua fell on his face to the earth, and did worship, and said unto him, What saith my lord unto his servant?* (Joshua 5:14 KJV)

*And the captain of the Lord's host said unto Joshua, Loose thy shoe from off thy foot; for the place whereon thou standest is holy. And Joshua did so* (Joshua 5:15 KJV).

*And he said, Hear thou therefore the word of the Lord: I saw the Lord sitting on His throne, and all the host of heaven standing by Him on His right hand and on His left* (1 Kings 22:19 KJV).

*For at that time day by day there came to David to help him, until it was a great host, like the host of God* (1 Chronicles 12:22 KJV).

*Again he said, Therefore hear the word of the Lord; I saw the Lord sitting upon His throne, and all the host of heaven standing on His right hand and on His left* (2 Chronicles 18:18 KJV).

*Thou, even Thou, art Lord alone; Thou hast made heaven, the heaven of heavens, with all their host, the earth, and all things that are therein, the seas, and all that is therein, and Thou preservest them all; and the host of heaven worshippeth Thee* (Nehemiah 9:6 KJV).

*By the word of the Lord were the heavens made; and all the host of them by the breath of His mouth* (Psalm 33:6 KJV).

*The noise of a multitude in the mountains, like as of a great people; a tumultuous noise of the kingdoms of nations gathered together: the Lord of hosts mustereth the host of the battle* (Isaiah 13:4 KJV).

*Lift up your eyes on high, and behold who hath created these things, that bringeth out their host by number: He calleth them all by names by the greatness of His might, for that He is strong in power; not one faileth* (Isaiah 40:26 KJV).

*I have made the earth, and created man upon it: I, even My hands, have stretched out the heavens, and all their host have I commanded* (Isaiah 45:12 KJV).

*As the host of heaven cannot be numbered, neither the sand of the sea measured: so will I multiply the seed of David My servant, and the Levites that minister unto Me* (Jeremiah 33:22 KJV).

*And when they went, I heard the noise of their wings, like the noise of great waters, as the voice of the Almighty, the voice of speech, as the noise of an host: when they stood, they let down their wings* (Ezekiel 1:24 KJV).

*And suddenly there was with the angel a multitude of the heavenly host praising God, and saying, Glory to God in the highest...* (Luke 2:13-14 KJV).

## Phrase: GABRIEL

*And I heard a man's voice between the banks of Ulai, which called, and said, Gabriel, make this man to understand the vision* (Daniel 8:16 KJV).

*Yea, whiles I was speaking in prayer, even the man Gabriel, whom I had seen in the vision at the beginning, being caused to fly swiftly, touched me about the time of the evening oblation* (Daniel 9:21 KJV).

*And the angel answering said unto him, I am Gabriel, that stand in the presence of God; and am sent to speak unto thee, and to shew thee these glad tidings* (Luke 1:19 KJV).

*And in the sixth month the angel Gabriel was sent from God unto a city of Galilee, named Nazareth* (Luke 1:26 KJV).

### Phrase: LUCIFER

*How art thou fallen from heaven, O Lucifer, son of the morning! how art thou cut down to the ground, which didst weaken the nations!* (Isaiah 14:12 KJV).

### Phrase: MICHAEL

*But the prince of the kingdom of Persia withstood me one and twenty days: but, lo, Michael, one of the chief princes, came to help me; and I remained there with the kings of Persia* (Daniel 10:13 KJV).

*But I will shew thee that which is noted in the scripture of truth: and there is none that holdeth with me in these things, but Michael your prince* (Daniel 10:21 KJV).

*And at that time shall Michael stand up, the great prince which standeth for the children of thy people: and there shall be a time of trouble, such as never was since there was a nation even to that same time: and at that time thy people shall be delivered, every one that shall be found written in the book* (Daniel 12:1 KJV).

*Yet Michael the archangel, when contending with the devil he disputed about the body of Moses, durst not bring against him a railing accusation, but said, The Lord rebuke thee* (Jude 1:9 KJV).

*And there was war in heaven: Michael and his angels fought against the dragon; and the dragon fought and his angels* (Revelation 12:7 KJV).

## Phrase: ARCHANGEL

*For the Lord Himself shall descend from heaven with a shout, with the voice of the archangel, and with the trump of God: and the dead in Christ shall rise first* (1 Thessalonians 4:16 KJV).

*Yet Michael the archangel, when contending with the devil he disputed about the body of Moses, durst not bring against him a railing accusation, but said, The Lord rebuke thee* (Jude 1:9 KJV).

## Phrase: HEAVENLY HOST

*And suddenly there was with the angel a multitude of the heavenly host praising God, and saying, Glory to God in the highest...* (Luke 2:13-14 KJV).

## Phrase: ANGELS

*And there came two angels to Sodom at even; and Lot sat in the gate of Sodom: and Lot seeing them rose up to meet them; and he bowed himself with his face toward the ground* (Genesis 19:1 KJV).

*And when the morning arose, then the angels hastened Lot, saying, Arise, take thy wife, and thy two daughters, which are here; lest thou be consumed in the iniquity of the city* (Genesis 19:15 KJV).

*And he dreamed, and behold a ladder set up on the earth, and the top of it reached to heaven: and behold the angels of God ascending and descending on it* (Genesis 28:12 KJV).

*And Jacob went on his way, and the angels of God met him* (Genesis 32:1 KJV).

*Behold, He put no trust in His servants; and His angels He charged with folly* (Job 4:18 KJV).

*For Thou hast made him a little lower than the angels, and hast crowned him with glory and honour* (Psalm 8:5 KJV).

*The chariots of God are twenty thousand, even thousands of angels: the Lord is among them, as in Sinai, in the holy place* (Psalm 68:17 KJV).

*Man did eat angels' food: He sent them meat to the full* (Psalm 78:25 KJV).

*He cast upon them the fierceness of His anger, wrath, and indignation, and trouble, by sending evil angels among them* (Psalm 78:49 KJV).

*For He shall give His angels charge over thee, to keep thee in all thy ways* (Psalm 91:11 KJV).

*Bless the Lord, ye His angels, that excel in strength, that do His commandments, hearkening unto the voice of His word* (Psalm 103:20 KJV).

*Who maketh His angels spirits; His ministers a flaming fire* (Psalm 104:4 KJV).

*Praise ye Him, all His angels: praise ye Him, all His hosts* (Psalm 148:2 KJV).

*And saith unto Him, If Thou be the Son of God, cast Thyself down: for it is written, He shall give His angels charge concerning Thee: and in their hands they shall bear Thee up, lest at any time Thou dash Thy foot against a stone* (Matthew 4:6 KJV).

*Then the devil leaveth Him, and, behold, angels came and ministered unto Him* (Matthew 4:11 KJV).

*The enemy that sowed them is the devil; the harvest is the end of the world; and the reapers are the angels* (Matthew 13:39 KJV).

*The Son of man shall send forth His angels, and they shall gather out of His kingdom all things that offend, and them which do iniquity* (Matthew 13:41 KJV).

*So shall it be at the end of the world: the angels shall come forth, and sever the wicked from among the just* (Matthew 13:49 KJV).

*For the Son of man shall come in the glory of His Father with His angels; and then He shall reward every man according to his works* (Matthew 16:27 KJV).

*Take heed that ye despise not one of these little ones; for I say unto you, That in heaven their angels do always behold the face of My Father which is in heaven* (Matthew 18:10 KJV).

*For in the resurrection they neither marry, nor are given in marriage, but are as the angels of God in heaven* (Matthew 22:30 KJV).

*And He shall send His angels with a great sound of a trumpet, and they shall gather together His elect from the four winds, from one end of heaven to the other* (Matthew 24:31 KJV).

*But of that day and hour knoweth no man, no, not the angels of heaven, but My Father only* (Matthew 24:36 KJV).

*When the Son of man shall come in His glory, and all the holy angels with Him, then shall He sit upon the throne of His glory* (Matthew 25:31 KJV).

*Then shall He say also unto them on the left hand, Depart from Me, ye cursed, into everlasting fire, prepared for the devil and His angels* (Matthew 25:41 KJV).

*Thinkest thou that I cannot now pray to My Father, and He shall presently give Me more than twelve legions of angels?* (Matthew 26:53 KJV)

*And He was there in the wilderness forty days, tempted of Satan; and was with the wild beasts; and the angels ministered unto Him* (Mark 1:13 KJV).

*Whosoever therefore shall be ashamed of Me and of My words in this adulterous and sinful generation; of him also shall the Son of man be ashamed, when He cometh in the glory of His Father with the holy angels* (Mark 8:38 KJV).

*For when they shall rise from the dead, they neither marry, nor are given marriage; but are as the angels which are in heaven* (Mark 12:25 KJV).

*And then shall He send His angels, and shall gather together His elect from the four winds, from the uttermost part of the earth to the uttermost part of heaven* (Mark 13:27 KJV).

*But of that day and that hour knoweth no man, no, not the angels which are in heaven, neither the Son, but the Father* (Mark 13:32 KJV).

*And it came to pass, as the angels were gone away from them into heaven, the shepherds said one to another, Let us now go even unto Bethlehem, and see this thing which is come to pass, which the Lord hath made known unto us* (Luke 2:15 KJV).

*For it is written, He shall give His angels charge over thee, to keep thee* (Luke 4:10 KJV).

*For whosoever shall be ashamed of Me and of My words, of him shall the Son of man be ashamed, when He shall come in His own glory, and in His Father's, and of the holy angels* (Luke 9:26 KJV).

*Also I say unto you, Whosoever shall confess Me before men, him shall the Son of man also confess before the angels of God* (Luke 12:8 KJV).

*But he that denieth Me before men shall be denied before the angels of God* (Luke 12:9 KJV).

*Likewise, I say unto you, there is joy in the presence of the angels of God over one sinner that repenteth* (Luke 15:10 KJV).

*And it came to pass, that the beggar died, and was carried by the angels into Abraham's bosom: the rich man also died, and was buried* (Luke 16:22 KJV).

*Neither can they die any more: for they are equal unto the angels; and are the children of God, being the children of the resurrection* (Luke 20:36 KJV).

*And when they found not His body, they came, saying, that they had also seen a vision of angels, which said that He was alive* (Luke 24:23 KJV).

*And He saith unto him, Verily, verily, I say unto you, Hereafter ye shall see heaven open, and the angels of God ascending and descending upon the Son of man* (John 1:51 KJV).

*And seeth two angels in white sitting, the one at the head, and the other at the feet, where the body of Jesus had lain* (John 20:12 KJV).

*Who have received the law by the disposition of angels, and have not kept it* (Acts 7:53 KJV).

*For I am persuaded, that neither death, nor life, nor angels, nor principalities, nor powers, nor things present, nor things to come... shall be able to separate us from the love of God...in Christ Jesus our Lord* (Romans 8:38-39 KJV).

*For I think that God hath set forth us the apostles last, as it were appointed to death: for we are made a spectacle unto the world, and to angels, and to men* (I Corinthians 4:9 KJV).

*Know ye not that we shall judge angels? How much more things that pertain to this life?* (I Corinthians 6:3 KJV)

*For this cause ought the woman to have power on her head because of the angels* (I Corinthians 11:10 KJV).

*Though I speak with the tongues of men and of angels, and have not charity, I am become as sounding brass, or a tinkling cymbal* (I Corinthians 13:1 KJV).

*Wherefore then serveth the law? It was added because of transgressions, till the seed should come to whom the promise was made; and it was ordained by angels in the hand of a mediator* (Galatians 3:19 KJV).

*Let no man beguile you of your reward in a voluntary humility and worshipping of angels, intruding into those things which he hath not seen, vainly puffed up by his fleshly mind* (Colossians 2:18 KJV).

*And to you who are troubled rest with us, when the Lord Jesus shall be revealed from heaven with His mighty angels* (2 Thessalonians 1:7 KJV).

*And without controversy great is the mystery of godliness: God was manifest in the flesh, justified in the Spirit, seen of angels, preached unto the Gentiles, believed on in the world, received up into glory* (1 Timothy 3:16 KJV).

*I charge thee before God, and the Lord Jesus Christ, and the elect angels, that thou observe these things without preferring one before another, doing nothing by partiality* (1 Timothy 5:21 KJV).

*Being made so much better than the angels, as He hath by inheritance obtained a more excellent name than they* (Hebrews 1:4 KJV).

*For unto which of the angels said He at any time, Thou art My Son, this day have I begotten Thee? And again, I will be to Him a Father, and He shall be to Me a Son?* (Hebrews 1:5 KJV)

*And again, when He bringeth in the firstbegotten into the world, He saith, And let all the angels of God worship Him* (Hebrews 1:6 KJV).

*And of the angels He saith, Who maketh His angels spirits, and His ministers a flame of fire* (Hebrews 1:7 KJV).

*But to which of the angels said He at any time, Sit on My right hand, until I make thine enemies thy footstool?* (Hebrews 1:13 KJV)

*For if the word spoken by angels was stedfast, and every transgression and disobedience received a just recompence of reward* (Hebrews 2:2 KJV).

*For unto the angels hath He not put in subjection the world to come, whereof we speak* (Hebrews 2:5 KJV).

*Thou madest him a little lower than the angels; Thou crownedst him with glory and honour, and didst set him over the works of Thy hands* (Hebrews 2:7 KJV).

*But we see Jesus, who was made a little lower than the angels for the suffering of death, crowned with glory and honour; that He by the grace of God should taste death for every man* (Hebrews 2:9 KJV).

*For verily He took not on Him the nature of angels; but He took on Him the seed of Abraham* (Hebrews 2:16 KJV).

*But ye are come unto mount Sion, and unto the city of the living God, the heavenly Jerusalem, and to an innumerable company of angels* (Hebrews 12:22 KJV).

*Be not forgetful to entertain strangers: for thereby some have entertained angels unawares* (Hebrews 13:2 KJV).

*Unto whom it was revealed, that not unto themselves, but unto us they did minister the things, which are now reported unto you by them that have preached the gospel unto you with the Holy Ghost sent down from heaven; which things the angels desire to look into* (1 Peter 1:12 KJV).

*Who is gone into heaven, and is on the right hand of God; angels and authorities and powers being made subject unto Him* (1 Peter 3:22 KJV).

*For if God spared not the angels that sinned, but cast them down to hell, and delivered them into chains of darkness, to be reserved unto judgment* (2 Peter 2:4 KJV).

*Whereas angels, which are greater in power and might, bring not railing accusation against them before the Lord* (2 Peter 2:11 KJV).

*And the angels which kept not their first estate, but left their own habitation, He hath reserved in everlasting chains under darkness unto the judgment of the great day* (Jude 1:6 KJV).

*The mystery of the seven stars which thou sawest in My right hand, and the seven golden candlesticks. The seven stars are the angels of the seven churches: and the seven candlesticks which thou sawest are the seven churches* (Revelation 1:20 KJV).

*He that overcometh, the same shall be clothed in white raiment; and I will not blot out his name out of the book of life, but I will confess his name before My Father, and before His angels* (Revelation 3:5 KJV).

*And I beheld, and I heard the voice of many angels round about the throne and the beasts and the elders: and the number of them was ten thousand times ten thousand, and thousands of thousands* (Revelation 5:11 KJV).

*And after these things I saw four angels standing on the four corners of the earth, holding the four winds of the earth, that the wind should not blow on the earth, nor on the sea, nor on any tree* (Revelation 7:1 KJV).

*And I saw another angel ascending from the east, having the seal of the living God: and he cried with a loud voice to the four angels, to whom it was given to hurt the earth and the sea* (Revelation 7:2 KJV).

*And all the angels stood round about the throne, and about the elders and the four beasts, and fell before the throne on their faces, and worshipped God* (Revelation 7:11 KJV).

*And I saw the seven angels which stood before God; and to them were given seven trumpets* (Revelation 8:2 KJV).

*And the seven angels which had the seven trumpets prepared themselves to sound* (Revelation 8:6 KJV).

*And I beheld, and heard an angel flying through the midst of heaven, saying with a loud voice, Woe, woe, woe, to the inhabiters of the earth by reason of the other voices of the trumpet of the three angels, which are yet to sound!* (Revelation 8:13 KJV).

*Saying to the sixth angel which had the trumpet, Loose the four angels which are bound in the great river Euphrates* (Revelation 9:14 KJV).

*And the four angels were loosed, which were prepared for an hour, and a day, and a month, and a year, for to slay the third part of men* (Revelation 9:15 KJV).

*And there was war in heaven: Michael and his angels fought against the dragon; and the dragon fought and his angels* (Revelation 12:7 KJV).

*And the great dragon was cast cut, that old serpent, called the Devil, and Satan, which deceiveth the whole world: he was cast out into the earth, and his angels were cast out with him* (Revelation 12:9 KJV).

*The same shall drink of the wine of the wrath of God, which is poured out without mixture into the cup of His indignation; and he shall be tormented with fire and brimstone in the presence of the holy angels, and in the presence of the Lamb* (Revelation 14:10 KJV).

*And I saw another sign in heaven, great and marvellous, seven angels having the seven last plagues; for in them is filled up the wrath of God* (Revelation 15:1 KJV).

*And the seven angels came out of the temple, having the seven plagues, clothed in pure and white linen, and having their breasts girded with golden girdles* (Revelation 15:6 KJV).

*And one of the four beasts gave unto the seven angels seven golden vials full of the wrath of God, who liveth for ever and ever* (Revelation 15:7 KJV).

*And the temple was filled with smoke from the glory of God, and from His power; and no man was able to enter into the temple, till the seven plagues of the seven angels were fulfilled* (Revelation 15:8 KJV).

*And I heard a great voice out of the temple saying to the seven angels, Go your ways, and pour out the vials of the wrath of God upon the earth* (Revelation 16:1 KJV).

*And there came one of the seven angels which had the seven vials, and talked with me, saying unto me, Come hither; I will shew unto thee the judgment of the great whore that sitteth upon many waters* (Revelation 17:1 KJV).

*And there came unto me one of the seven angels which had the seven vials full of the seven last plagues, and talked with me, saying, Come hither, I will shew thee the bride, the Lamb's wife* (Revelation 21:9 KJV).

*And had a wall great and high, and had twelve gates, and at the gates twelve angels, and names written thereon, which are the names of the twelve tribes of the children of Israel* (Revelation 21:12 KJV).

**Phrase: ANGEL**

*And the angel of the Lord found her by a fountain of water in the wilderness, by the fountain in the way to Shur* (Genesis 16:7 KJV).

*And the angel of the Lord said unto her, Return to thy mistress, and submit thyself under her hands* (Genesis 16:9 KJV).

*And the angel of the Lord said unto her, I will multiply thy seed exceedingly, that it shall not be numbered for multitude* (Genesis 16:10 KJV).

*And the angel of the Lord said unto her, Behold, thou art with child and shalt bear a son, and shalt call his name Ishmael; because the Lord hath heard thy affliction* (Genesis 16:11 KJV).

*And God heard the voice of the lad; and the angel of God called to Hagar out of heaven, and said unto her, What aileth thee, Hagar? fear not; for God hath heard the voice of the lad where he is* (Genesis 21:17 KJV).

*And the angel of the Lord called unto him out of heaven, and said, Abraham, Abraham: and he said, Here am I* (Genesis 22:11 KJV).

*And the angel of the Lord called unto Abraham out of heaven the second time* (Genesis 22:15 KJV).

*The Lord God of heaven, which took me from my father's house, and from the land of my kindred, and which spake unto me, and that sware unto me, saying, Unto thy seed will I give this land; He shall send His angel before thee, and thou shalt take a wife unto my son from thence* (Genesis 24:7 KJV).

*And he said unto me, The Lord, before whom I walk, will send His angel with thee, and prosper thy way; and thou shalt take a wife for my son of my kindred, and of my father's house* (Genesis 24:40 KJV).

*And the angel of God spake unto me in a dream, saying, Jacob: And I said, Here am I* (Genesis 31:11 KJV).

*The Angel which redeemed me from all evil, bless the lads; and let my name be named on them, and the name of my fathers Abraham and Isaac; and let them grow into a multitude in the midst of the earth* (Genesis 48:16 KJV).

*And the angel of the Lord appeared unto him in a flame of fire out of the midst of a bush: and he looked, and, behold, the bush burned with fire, and the bush was not consumed* (Exodus 3:2 KJV).

*And the angel of God, which went before the camp of Israel, removed and went behind them; and the pillar of the cloud went from before their face, and stood behind them* (Exodus 14:19 KJV).

*Behold, I send an angel before thee, to keep thee in the way, and to bring thee into the place which I have prepared* (Exodus 23:20 KJV).

*For mine Angel shall go before thee, and bring thee in unto the Amorites, and the Hittites, and the Perizzites, and the Canaanites, the Hivites, and the Jebusites: and I will cut them off* (Exodus 23:23 KJV).

*Therefore now go, lead the people unto the place of which I have spoken unto thee: behold, Mine Angel shall go before thee: nevertheless in the day when I visit I will visit their sin upon them* (Exodus 32:34 KJV).

*And I will send an angel before thee; and I will drive out the Canaanite, the Amorite, and the Hittite, and the Perizzite, the Hivite, and the Jebusite* (Exodus 33:2 KJV).

*And when we cried unto the Lord, He heard our voice, and sent an angel, and hath brought us forth out of Egypt: and, behold, we are in Kadesh, a city in the uttermost of thy border* (Numbers 20:16 KJV).

*And God's anger was kindled because he went: and the angel of the Lord stood in the way for an adversary against him. Now he was riding upon his ass, and his two servants were with him* (Numbers 22:22 KJV).

*And the ass saw the angel of the Lord standing in the way, and his sword drawn in his hand: and the ass turned aside out of the way, and went into the field: and Balaam smote the ass, to turn her into the way* (Numbers 22:23 KJV).

*But the angel of the Lord stood in a path of the vineyards, a wall being on this side, and a wall on that side* (Numbers 22:24 KJV).

*And when the ass saw the angel of the Lord, she thrust herself unto the wall, and crushed Balaam's foot against the wall: and he smote her again* (Numbers 22:25 KJV).

*And the angel of the Lord went further, and stood in a narrow place, where was no way to turn either to the right hand or to the left* (Numbers 22:26 KJV).

*And when the ass saw the angel of the Lord, she fell down under Balaam: and Balaam's anger was kindled, and he smote the ass with a staff* (Numbers 22:27 KJV).

*Then the Lord opened the eyes of Balaam, and he saw the angel of the Lord standing in the way, and his sword drawn in his hand: and he bowed down his head, and fell flat on his face* (Numbers 22:31 KJV).

*And the angel of the Lord said unto him, Wherefore hast thou smitten thine ass these three times? Behold, I went out to withstand thee, because thy way is perverse before me* (Numbers 22:32 KJV).

*And Balaam said unto the angel of the Lord, I have sinned; for I knew not that thou stoodest in the way against me: Now therefore, if it displease thee, I will get me back again* (Numbers 22:34 KJV).

*And the angel of the Lord said unto Balaam, Go with the men: but only the word that I shall speak unto thee, that thou shalt speak. So Balaam went with the princes of Balak* (Numbers 22:35 KJV).

*And an angel of the Lord came up from Gilgal to Bochim, and said, I made you to go up out of Egypt, and have brought you unto the land which I sware unto your fathers; and I said, I will never break my covenant with you* (Judges 2:1 KJV).

*And it came to pass, when the angel of the Lord spake these words unto all the children of Israel, that the people lifted up their voice, and wept* (Judges 2:4 KJV).

*Curse ye Meroz, said the angel of the Lord, curse ye bitterly the inhabitants thereof; because they came not to the help of the Lord, to the help of the Lord against the mighty* (Judges 5:23 KJV).

*And there came an angel of the Lord, and sat under an oak which was in Ophrah, that pertained unto Joash the Abiezrite: and his* son Gideon threshed wheat by the winepress, to hide it from the Midianites (Judges 6:11 KJV).

And the angel of the Lord appeared unto him, and said unto him, The Lord is with thee, thou mighty man of valour (Judges 6:12 KJV).

And the angel of God said unto him, Take the flesh and the unleavened cakes, and lay them upon this rock, and pour out the broth. And he did so (Judges 6:20 KJV).

Then the angel of the Lord put forth the end of the staff that was in his hand, and touched the flesh and the unleavened cakes; and there rose up fire out of the rock, and consumed the flesh and the unleavened cakes. Then the angel of the Lord departed out of his sight (Judges 6:21 KJV).

And when Gideon perceived that he was an angel of the Lord, Gideon said, Alas, O Lord God! For because I have seen an angel of the Lord face to face (Judges 6:22 KJV).

And the angel of the Lord appeared unto the woman, and said unto her, Behold now, thou art barren, and bearest not: but thou shalt conceive, and bear a son (Judges 13:3 KJV).

Then the woman came and told her husband, saying, A man of God came unto me, and his countenance was like the countenance of an angel of God, very terrible: but I asked him not whence he was, neither told he me his name (Judges 13:6 KJV).

And God hearkened to the voice of Manoah; and the angel of God came again unto the woman as she sat in the field: but Manoah her husband was not with her (Judges 13:9 KJV).

*And the angel of the Lord said unto Manoah, Of all that I said unto the woman let her beware* (Judges 13:13 KJV).

*And Manoah said unto the angel of the Lord, I pray thee, let us detain thee, until we shall have made ready a kid for thee* (Judges 13:15 KJV).

*And the angel of the Lord said unto Manoah, Though thou detain me, I will not eat of thy bread: and if thou wilt offer a burnt offering, thou must offer it unto the Lord. For Manoah knew not that he was an angel of the Lord* (Judges 13:16 KJV).

*And Manoah said unto the angel of the Lord, What is thy name, that when thy sayings come to pass we may do thee honour?* (Judges 13:17 KJV)

*And the angel of the Lord said unto him, Why askest thou thus after my name, seeing it is secret?* (Judges 13:18 KJV)

*So Manoah took a kid with a meat offering, and offered it upon a rock unto the Lord: and the angel did wondrously; and Manoah and his wife looked on* (Judges 13:19 KJV).

*For it came to pass, when the flame went up toward heaven from off the altar, that the angel of the Lord ascended in the flame of the altar. And Manoah and his wife looked on it, and fell on their faces to the ground* (Judges 13:20 KJV).

*But the angel of the Lord did no more appear to Manoah and to his wife. Then Manoah knew that he was an angel of the Lord* (Judges 13:21 KJV).

*And Achish answered and said to David, I know that thou art good in my sight, as an angel of God: notwithstanding the princes of the Philistines have said, He shall not go up with us to the battle* (1 Samuel 29:9 KJV).

*Then thine handmaid said, The word of my lord the king shall now be comfortable: for as an angel of God, so is my lord the king to discern good and bad: therefore the Lord thy God will be with thee* (2 Samuel 14:17 KJV).

*To fetch about this form of speech hath thy servant Joab done this thing: and my lord is wise, according to the wisdom of an angel of God, to know all things that are in the earth* (2 Samuel 14:20 KJV).

*And he hath slandered thy servant unto my lord the king; but my lord the king is as an angel of God: do therefore what is good in thine eyes* (2 Samuel 19:27 KJV).

*And when the angel stretched out his hand upon Jerusalem to destroy it, the Lord repented Him of the evil, and said to the angel that destroyed the people, It is enough: stay now thine hand. And the angel of the Lord was by the threshingplace of Araunah the Jebusite* (2 Samuel 24:16 KJV).

*And David spake unto the Lord when he saw the angel that smote the people, and said, Lo, I have sinned, and I have done wickedly: but these sheep, what have they done? let Thine hand, I pray Thee, be against me, and against my father's house* (2 Samuel 24:17 KJV).

*He said unto him, I am a prophet also as thou art; and an angel spake unto me by the word of the Lord, saying, Bring him back with thee into thine house, that he may eat bread and drink water. But he lied unto him* (1 Kings 13:18 KJV).

*And as he lay and slept under a juniper tree, behold, then an angel touched him, and said unto him, Arise and eat* (I Kings 19:5 KJV).

*And the angel of the Lord came again the second time, and touched him, and said, Arise and eat; because the journey is too great for thee* (I Kings 19:7 KJV).

*But the angel of the Lord said to Elijah the Tishbite, Arise, go up to meet the messengers of the king of Samaria, and say unto them, Is it not because there is not a God in Israel, that ye go to inquire of Baalzebub the god of Ekron?* (2 Kings 1:3 KJV).

*And the angel of the Lord said unto Elijah, Go down with him: be not afraid of him. And he arose, and went down with him unto the king* (2 Kings 1:15 KJV).

*And it came to pass that night, that the angel of the Lord went out, and smote in the camp of the Assyrians an hundred fourscore and five thousand: and when they arose early in the morning, behold, they were all dead corpses* (2 Kings 19:35 KJV).

*Either three years' famine; or three months to be destroyed before thy foes, while that the sword of thine enemies overtaketh thee; or else three days the sword of the Lord, even the pestilence, in the land, and the angel of the Lord destroying throughout all the coasts of Israel. Now therefore advise thyself what word I shall bring again to Him that sent me* (I Chronicles 21:12 KJV).

*And God sent an angel unto Jerusalem to destroy it: and as he was destroying, the Lord beheld, and He repented Him of the evil, and said to the angel that destroyed, It is enough, stay now thine hand. And the angel of the Lord stood by the threshingfloor of Ornan the Jebusite* (I Chronicles 21:15 KJV).

*And David lifted up his eyes, and saw the angel of the Lord stand between the earth and the heaven, having a drawn sword in his hand stretched out over Jerusalem. Then David and the elders of Israel, who were clothed in sackcloth, fell upon their faces* (1 Chronicles 21:16 KJV).

*Then the angel of the Lord commanded Gad to say to David, that David should go up, and set up an altar unto the Lord in the threshingfloor of Ornan the Jebusite* (1 Chronicles 21:18 KJV).

*And Ornan turned back, and saw the angel; and his four sons with him hid themselves. Now Ornan was threshing wheat* (1 Chronicles 21:20 KJV).

*And the Lord commanded the angel; and he put up his sword again into the sheath thereof* (1 Chronicles 21:27 KJV).

*But David could not go before it to enquire of God: for he was afraid because of the sword of the angel of the Lord* (1 Chronicles 21:30 KJV).

*And the Lord sent an angel, which cut off all the mighty men of valour, and the leaders and captains in the camp of the king of Assyria. So he returned with shame of face to his own land. And when he was come into the house of his god, they that came forth of his own bowels slew him there with the sword* (2 Chronicles 32:21 KJV).

*The angel of the Lord encampeth round about them that fear Him, and delivereth them* (Psalm 34:7 KJV).

*Let them be as chaff before the wind: and let the angel of the Lord chase them* (Psalm 35:5 KJV).

*Let their way be dark and slippery: and let the angel of the Lord persecute them* (Psalm 35:6 KJV).

*Suffer not thy mouth to cause thy flesh to sin; neither say thou before the angel, that it was an error: wherefore should God be angry at thy voice, and destroy the work of thine hands?* (Ecclesiastes 5:6 KJV)

*Then the angel of the Lord went forth, and smote in the camp of the Assyrians a hundred and fourscore and five thousand: and when they arose early in the morning, behold, they were all dead corpses* (Isaiah 37:36 KJV).

*In all their affliction He was afflicted, and the angel of His presence saved them: in His love and in His pity He redeemed them; and He bare them, and carried them all the days of old* (Isaiah 63:9 KJV).

*Then Nebuchadnezzar spake, and said, Blessed be the God of Shadrach, Meshach, and Abednego, who hath sent His angel, and delivered His servants that trusted in Him, and have changed the king's word, and yielded their bodies, that they might not serve nor worship any god, except their own God* (Daniel 3:28 KJV).

*My God hath sent His angel, and hath shut the lions' mouths, that they have not hurt me: forasmuch as before Him innocency was found in me; and also before thee, O king, have I done no hurt* (Daniel 6:22 KJV).

*Yea, he had power over the angel, and prevailed: he wept, and made supplication unto Him: he found Him in Bethel, and there He spake with us* (Hosea 12:4 KJV).

*Then said I, O my Lord, what are these? And the angel that talked with me said unto me, I will shew thee what these be* (Zechariah 1:9 KJV).

*And they answered the angel of the Lord that stood among the myrtle trees, and said, We have walked to and fro through the earth, and, behold, all the earth sitteth still, and is at rest* (Zechariah 1:11 KJV).

*Then the angel of the Lord answered and said, O Lord of hosts, how long wilt Thou not have mercy on Jerusalem and on the cities of Judah, against which Thou hast had indignation these threescore and ten years?* (Zechariah 1:12 KJV)

*And the Lord answered the angel that talked with me with good words and comfortable words* (Zechariah 1:13 KJV).

*So the angel that communed with me said unto me, Cry thou, saying, Thus saith the Lord of hosts; I am jealous for Jerusalem and for Zion with a great jealousy* (Zechariah 1:14 KJV).

*And I said unto the angel that talked with me, What be these? And he answered me, These are the horns which have scattered Judah, Israel, and Jerusalem* (Zechariah 1:19 KJV).

*And, behold, the angel that talked with me went forth, and another angel went out to meet him* (Zechariah 2:3 KJV).

*And he shewed me Joshua the high priest standing before the angel of the Lord, and Satan standing at his right hand to resist him* (Zechariah 3:1 KJV).

*Now Joshua was clothed with filthy garments, and stood before the angel* (Zechariah 3:3 KJV).

*And I said, Let them set a fair mitre upon his head. So they set a fair mitre upon his head, and clothed him with garments. And the angel of the Lord stood by* (Zechariah 3:5 KJV).

*And the angel of the Lord protested unto Joshua, saying, Thus saith the Lord of hosts...* (Zechariah 3:6-7 KJV).

*And the angel that talked with me came again, and waked me, as a man that is wakened out of his sleep* (Zechariah 4:1 KJV).

*So I answered and spake to the angel that talked with me, saying, What are these, my lord?* (Zechariah 4:4 KJV)

*Then the angel that talked with me answered and said unto me, Knowest thou not what these be? And I said, No, my lord* (Zechariah 4:5 KJV).

*Then the angel that talked with me went forth, and said unto me, Lift up now thine eyes, and see what is this that goeth forth* (Zechariah 5:5 KJV).

*Then said I to the angel that talked with me, Whither do these bear the ephah?* (Zechariah 5:10 KJV)

*Then I answered and said unto the angel that talked with me, What are these, my lord?* (Zechariah 6:4 KJV)

*And the angel answered and said unto me, These are the four spirits of the heavens, which go forth from standing before the Lord of all the earth* (Zechariah 6:5 KJV).

*In that day shall the Lord defend the inhabitants of Jerusalem; and he that is feeble among them at that day shall be as David; and the house of David shall be as God, as the angel of the Lord before them* (Zechariah 12:8 KJV).

*But while he thought on these things, behold, the angel of the Lord appeared unto him in a dream, saying, Joseph, thou son of David, fear not to take unto thee Mary thy wife: for that which is conceived in her is of the Holy Ghost* (Matthew 1:20 KJV).

*Then Joseph being raised from sleep did as the angel of the Lord had bidden him, and took unto him his wife* (Matthew 1:24 KJV).

*And when they were departed, behold, the angel of the Lord appeareth to Joseph in a dream, saying, Arise, and take the young child and his mother, and flee into Egypt, and be thou there until I bring thee word: for Herod will seek the young child to destroy Him* (Matthew 2:13 KJV).

*But when Herod was dead, behold, an angel of the Lord appeareth in a dream to Joseph in Egypt* (Matthew 2:19 KJV).

*And, behold, there was a great earthquake: for the angel of the Lord descended from heaven, and came and rolled back the stone from the door, and sat upon it* (Matthew 28:2 KJV).

*And the angel answered and said unto the women, Fear not ye: for I know that ye seek Jesus, which was crucified* (Matthew 28:5 KJV).

*And there appeared unto him an angel of the Lord standing on the right side of the altar of incense* (Luke 1:11 KJV).

*But the angel said unto him, Fear not, Zacharias: for thy prayer is heard; and thy wife Elisabeth shall bear thee a son, and thou shalt call his name John* (Luke 1:13 KJV).

*And Zacharias said unto the angel, Whereby shall I know this? for I am an old man, and my wife well stricken in years* (Luke 1:18 KJV).

*And the angel answering said unto him, I am Gabriel, that stand in the presence of God; and am sent to speak unto thee, and to shew thee these glad tidings* (Luke 1:19 KJV).

*And in the sixth month the angel Gabriel was sent from God unto a city of Galilee, named Nazareth* (Luke 1:26 KJV).

*And the angel came in unto her, and said, Hail, thou that art highly favoured, the Lord is with thee: blessed art thou among women* (Luke 1:28 KJV).

*And the angel said unto her, Fear not, Mary: for thou hast found favour with God* (Luke 1:30 KJV).

*Then said Mary unto the angel, How shall this be, seeing I know not a man?* (Luke 1:34 KJV)

*And the angel answered and said unto her, The Holy Ghost shall come upon thee, and the power of the Highest shall overshadow thee: therefore also that Holy Thing which shall be born of thee shall be called the Son of God* (Luke 1:35 KJV).

*And Mary said, Behold the handmaid of the Lord; be it unto me according to thy word. And the angel departed from her* (Luke 1:38 KJV).

*And, lo, the angel of the Lord came upon them, and the glory of the Lord shone round about them: and they were sore afraid* (Luke 2:9 KJV).

*And the angel said unto them, Fear not: for, behold, I bring you good tidings of great joy, which shall be to all people* (Luke 2:10 KJV).

*And suddenly there was with the angel a multitude of the heavenly host praising God, and saying, Glory to God in the highest...* (Luke 2:13-14 KJV).

*And when eight days were accomplished for the circumcising of the child, His name was called Jesus, which was so named of the angel before He was conceived in the womb* (Luke 2:21 KJV).

*And there appeared an angel unto Him from heaven, strengthening Him* (Luke 22:43 KJV).

*For an angel went down at a certain season into the pool, and troubled the water: whosoever then first after the troubling of the water stepped in was made whole of whatsoever disease he had* (John 5:4 KJV).

*The people therefore, that stood by, and heard it, said that it thundered: others said, An angel spake to Him* (John 12:29 KJV).

*But the angel of the Lord by night opened the prison doors, and brought them forth, and said, Go, stand and speak in the temple to the people all the words of this life* (Acts 5:19-20 KJV).

*And all that sat in the council, looking stedfastly on him, saw his face as it had been the face of an angel* (Acts 6:15 KJV).

*And when forty years were expired, there appeared to him in the wilderness of mount Sina an angel of the Lord in a flame of fire in a bush* (Acts 7:30 KJV).

*This Moses whom they refused, saying, Who made thee a ruler and a judge? the same did God send to be a ruler and a deliverer by the hand of the angel which appeared to him in the bush* (Acts 7:35 KJV).

*This is he, that was in the church in the wilderness with the angel which spake to him in the mount Sina, and with our fathers: who received the lively oracles to give unto us* (Acts 7:38 KJV).

*And the angel of the Lord spake unto Philip, saying, Arise, and go toward the south unto the way that goeth down from Jerusalem unto Gaza, which is desert* (Acts 8:26 KJV).

*He saw in a vision evidently about the ninth hour of the day an angel of God coming in to him, and saying unto him, Cornelius* (Acts 10:3 KJV).

*And when the angel which spake unto Cornelius was departed, he called two of his household servants, and a devout soldier of them that waited on him continually* (Acts 10:7 KJV).

*And they said, Cornelius the centurion, a just man, and one that feareth God, and of good report among all the nation of the Jews, was warned from God by an holy angel to send for thee into his house, and to hear words of thee* (Acts 10:22 KJV).

*And he shewed us how he had seen an angel in his house, which stood and said unto him, Send men to Joppa, and call for Simon, whose surname is Peter* (Acts 11:13 KJV).

*And, behold, the angel of the Lord came upon him, and a light shined in the prison: and he smote Peter on the side, and raised him up, saying, Arise up quickly. And his chains fell off from his hands* (Acts 12:7 KJV).

*And the angel said unto him, Gird thyself, and bind on thy sandals. And so he did. And he saith unto him, Cast thy garment about thee, and follow me* (Acts 12:8 KJV).

*And he went out, and followed him; and wist not that it was true which was done by the angel; but thought he saw a vision* (Acts 12:9 KJV).

*When they were past the first and the second ward, they came unto the iron gate that leadeth unto the city; which opened to them of his own accord: and they went out, and passed on through one street; and forthwith the angel departed from him* (Acts 12:10 KJV).

*And when Peter was come to himself, he said, Now I know of a surety, that the Lord hath sent His angel, and hath delivered me out of the hand of Herod, and from all the expectation of the people of the Jews* (Acts 12:11 KJV).

*And they said unto her, Thou art mad. But she constantly affirmed that it was even so. Then said they, It is his angel* (Acts 12:15 KJV).

*And immediately the angel of the Lord smote him, because he gave not God the glory: and he was eaten of worms, and gave up the ghost* (Acts 12:23 KJV).

*For the Sadducees say that there is no resurrection, neither angel, nor spirit: but the Pharisees confess both* (Acts 23:8 KJV).

*And there arose a great cry: and the scribes that were of the Pharisees' part arose, and strove, saying, We find no evil in this man: but if a spirit or an angel hath spoken to him, let us not fight against God* (Acts 23:9 KJV).

*For there stood by me this night the angel of God, whose I am, and whom I serve* (Acts 27:23 KJV).

*And no marvel; for Satan himself is transformed into an angel of light* (2 Corinthians 11:14 KJV).

*But though we, or an angel from heaven, preach any other gospel unto you than that which we have preached unto you, let him be accursed* (Galatians 1:8 KJV).

*And my temptation which was in my flesh ye despised not, nor rejected; but received me as an angel of God, even as Christ Jesus* (Galatians 4:14 KJV).

*The Revelation of Jesus Christ, which God gave unto Him, to shew unto His servants things which must shortly come to pass; and He sent and signified it by His angel unto His servant John* (Revelation 1:1 KJV).

*Unto the angel of the church of Ephesus write; These things saith He that holdeth the seven stars in His right hand, who walketh in the midst of the seven golden candlesticks* (Revelation 2:1 KJV).

*And unto the angel of the church in Smyrna write; These things saith the first and the last, which was dead, and is alive* (Revelation 2:8 KJV).

*And to the angel of the church in Pergamos write; These things saith He which hath the sharp sword with two edges* (Revelation 2:12 KJV).

*And unto the angel of the church in Thyatira write; These things saith the Son of God, who hath His eyes like unto a flame of fire, and His feet are like fine brass* (Revelation 2:18 KJV).

*And unto the angel of the church in Sardis write; These things saith He that hath the seven Spirits of God, and the seven stars; I know thy works, that thou hast a name that thou livest, and art dead* (Revelation 3:1 KJV).

*And to the angel of the church in Philadelphia write; These things saith He that is holy, He that is true, He that hath the key of David, He that openeth, and no man shutteth; and shutteth, and no man openeth* (Revelation 3:7 KJV).

*And unto the angel of the church of the Laodiceans write; These things saith the Amen, the faithful and true witness, the beginning of the creation of God* (Revelation 3:14 KJV).

*And I saw a strong angel proclaiming with a loud voice, Who is worthy to open the book, and to loose the seals thereof?* (Revelation 5:2 KJV)

*And I saw another angel ascending from the east, having the seal of the living God: and he cried with a loud voice to the four angels, to whom it was given to hurt the earth and the sea* (Revelation 7:2 KJV).

*And another angel came and stood at the altar, having a golden censer; and there was given unto him much incense, that he should offer it with the prayers of all saints upon the golden altar which was before the throne* (Revelation 8:3 KJV).

*And the smoke of the incense, which came with the prayers of the saints, ascended up before God out of the angel's hand* (Revelation 8:4 KJV).

*And the angel took the censer, and filled it with fire of the altar, and cast it into the earth: and there were voices, and thunderings, and lightnings, and an earthquake* (Revelation 8:5 KJV).

*The first angel sounded, and there followed hail and fire mingled with blood, and they were cast upon the earth: and the third part of trees was burnt up, and all green grass was burnt up* (Revelation 8:7 KJV).

*And the second angel sounded, and as it were a great mountain burning with fire was cast into the sea: and the third part of the sea became blood* (Revelation 8:8 KJV).

*And the third angel sounded, and there fell a great star from heaven, burning as it were a lamp, and it fell upon the third part of the rivers, and upon the fountains of waters* (Revelation 8:10 KJV).

*And the fourth angel sounded, and the third part of the sun was smitten, and the third part of the moon, and the third part of the stars; so as the third part of them was darkened, and the day shone not for a third part of it, and the night likewise* (Revelation 8:12 KJV).

*And I beheld, and heard an angel flying through the midst of heaven, saying with a loud voice, Woe, woe, woe, to the inhabiters of the earth by reason of the other voices of the trumpet of the three angels, which are yet to sound!* (Revelation 8:13 KJV)

*And the fifth angel sounded, and I saw a star fall from heaven unto the earth: and to him was given the key of the bottomless pit* (Revelation 9:1 KJV).

*And they had a king over them, which is the angel of the bottomless pit, whose name in the Hebrew tongue is Abaddon, but in the Greek tongue hath his name Apollyon* (Revelation 9:11 KJV).

*And the sixth angel sounded, and I heard a voice from the four horns of the golden altar which is before God* (Revelation 9:13 KJV).

*Saying to the sixth angel which had the trumpet, Loose the four angels which are bound in the great river Euphrates* (Revelation 9:14 KJV).

*And I saw another mighty angel come down from heaven, clothed with a cloud: and a rainbow was upon his head, and his face was as it were the sun, and his feet as pillars of fire* (Revelation 10:1 KJV).

*And the angel which I saw stand upon the sea and upon the earth lifted up his hand to heaven* (Revelation 10:5 KJV).

*But in the days of the voice of the seventh angel, when he shall begin to sound, the mystery of God should be finished, as He hath declared to His servants the prophets* (Revelation 10:7 KJV).

*And the voice which I heard from heaven spake unto me again, and said, Go and take the little book which is open in the hand of the angel which standeth upon the sea and upon the earth* (Revelation 10:8 KJV).

*And I went unto the angel, and said unto him, Give me the little book. And he said unto me, Take it, and eat it up; and it shall make thy belly bitter, but it shall be in thy mouth sweet as honey* (Revelation 10:9 KJV).

*And I took the little book out of the angel's hand, and ate it up; and it was in my mouth sweet as honey: and as soon as I had eaten it, my belly was bitter* (Revelation 10:10 KJV).

*And there was given me a reed like unto a rod: and the angel stood, saying, Rise, and measure the temple of God, and the altar, and them that worship therein* (Revelation 11:1 KJV).

*And the seventh angel sounded; and there were great voices in heaven, saying, The kingdoms of this world are become the kingdoms of our Lord, and of His Christ; and He shall reign for ever and ever* (Revelation 11:15 KJV).

*And I saw another angel fly in the midst of heaven, having the everlasting gospel to preach unto them that dwell on the earth, and to every nation, and kindred, and tongue, and people* (Revelation 14:6 KJV).

*And there followed another angel, saying, Babylon is fallen, is fallen, the great city, because she made all nations drink of the wine of the wrath of her fornication* (Revelation 14:8 KJV).

*And the third angel followed them, saying with a loud voice, If any man worship the beast and his image, and receive his mark in his forehead, or in his hand* (Revelation 14:9 KJV).

*And another angel came out of the temple, crying with a loud voice to Him that sat on the cloud, Thrust in Thy sickle, and reap: for the time is come for Thee to reap; for the harvest of the earth is ripe* (Revelation 14:15 KJV).

*And another angel came out of the temple which is in heaven, he also having a sharp sickle* (Revelation 14:17 KJV).

*And another angel came out from the altar, which had power over fire; and cried with a loud cry to him that had the sharp sickle, saying, Thrust in thy sharp sickle, and gather the clusters of the vine of the earth; for her grapes are fully ripe* (Revelation 14:18 KJV).

*And the angel thrust in his sickle into the earth, and gathered the vine of the earth, and cast it into the great winepress of the wrath of God* (Revelation 14:19 KJV).

*And the second angel poured out his vial upon the sea; and it became as the blood of a dead man: and every living soul died in the sea* (Revelation 16:3 KJV).

*And the third angel poured out his vial upon the rivers and fountains of waters; and they became blood* (Revelation 16:4 KJV).

*And I heard the angel of the waters say, Thou art righteous, O Lord, which art, and wast, and shalt be, because Thou hast judged thus* (Revelation 16:5 KJV).

*And the fourth angel poured out his vial upon the sun; and power was given unto him to scorch men with fire* (Revelation 16:8 KJV).

*And the fifth angel poured out his vial upon the seat of the beast; and his kingdom was full of darkness; and they gnawed their tongues for pain* (Revelation 16:10 KJV).

*And the sixth angel poured out his vial upon the great river Euphrates; and the water thereof was dried up, that the way of the kings of the east might be prepared* (Revelation 16:12 KJV).

*And the seventh angel poured out his vial into the air; and there came a great voice out of the temple of heaven, from the throne, saying, It is done* (Revelation 16:17 KJV).

*And the angel said unto me, Wherefore didst thou marvel? I will tell thee the mystery of the woman, and of the beast that carrieth her, which hath the seven heads and ten horns* (Revelation 7:7 KJV).

*And after these things I saw another angel come down from heaven, having great power; and the earth was lightened with his glory* (Revelation 18:1 KJV).

*And a mighty angel took up a stone like a great millstone, and cast it in the sea, saying, Thus with violence shall that great city*

*Babylon be thrown down, and shall be found no more at all* (Revelation 18:21 KJV).

*And I saw an angel standing in the sun; and he cried with a loud voice, saying to all the fowls that fly in the midst of heaven, Come and gather yourselves together unto the supper of the great God* (Revelation 19:17 KJV).

*And I saw an angel come down from heaven, having the key of the bottomless pit and a great chain in his hand* (Revelation 20:1 KJV).

*And he measured the wall thereof, an hundred and forty and four cubits, according to the measure of a man, that is, of the angel* (Revelation 21:17 KJV).

*And he said unto me, These sayings are faithful and true: and the Lord God of the holy prophets sent His angel to shew unto His servants the things which must shortly be done* (Revelation 22:6 KJV).

*And I John saw these things, and heard them. And when I had heard and seen, I fell down to worship before the feet of the angel which shewed me these things* (Revelation 22:8 KJV).

*I Jesus have sent Mine angel to testify unto you these things in the churches. I am the root and the offspring of David, and the bright and morning star* (Revelation 22:16 KJV).

## Phrase: HOLY ONE

Authors' Note: When *Holy* One is capitalized, it is definitely in reference to the name of Jesus, the Holy One.

*And of Levi he said, Let Thy Thummim and Thy Urim be with Thy holy one, whom Thou didst prove at Massah, and with whom*

*Thou didst strive at the waters of Meribah* (Deuteronomy 33:8 KJV).

*Whom hast thou reproached and blasphemed? and against whom hast thou exalted thy voice, and lifted up thine eyes on high? even against the Holy One of Israel* (2 Kings 19:22 KJV).

*Then should I yet have comfort; yea, I would harden myself in sorrow: let Him not spare; for I have not concealed the words of the Holy One* (Job 6:10 KJV).

*For Thou wilt not leave my soul in hell; neither wilt Thou suffer Thine Holy One to see corruption* (Psalm 16:10 KJV).

*I will also praise Thee with the psaltery, even Thy truth, O my God: unto Thee will I sing with the harp, O Thou Holy One of Israel* (Psalm 71:22 KJV).

*Yea, they turned back and tempted God, and limited the Holy One of Israel* (Psalm 78:41 KJV).

*For the Lord is our defence; and the Holy One of Israel is our king* (Psalm 89:18 KJV).

*Then Thou spakest in vision to Thy holy one, and saidst, I have laid help upon one that is mighty; I have exalted one chosen out of the people* (Psalm 89:19 KJV).

*Ah sinful nation, a people laden with iniquity, a seed of evildoers, children that are corrupters: they have forsaken the Lord, they have provoked the Holy One of Israel unto anger, they are gone away backward* (Isaiah 1:4 KJV).

*That say, Let Him make speed, and hasten His work, that we may see it: and let the counsel of the Holy One of Israel draw nigh and come, that we may know it!* (Isaiah 5:19 KJV)

*Therefore as the fire devoureth the stubble, and the flame consumeth the chaff, so their root shall be as rottenness, and their blossom shall go up as dust: because they have cast away the law of the Lord of hosts, and despised the word of the Holy One of Israel* (Isaiah 5:24 KJV).

*And the light of Israel shall be for a fire, and His Holy One for a flame: and it shall burn and devour his thorns and his briers in one day* (Isaiah 10:17 KJV).

*And it shall come to pass in that day, that the remnant of Israel, and such as are escaped of the house of Jacob, shall no more again stay upon him that smote them; but shall stay upon the Lord, the Holy One of Israel, in truth* (Isaiah 10:20 KJV).

*Cry out and shout, thou inhabitant of Zion: for great is the Holy One of Israel in the midst of thee* (Isaiah 12:6 KJV).

*At that day shall man look to his Maker, and his eyes shall have respect to the Holy One of Israel* (Isaiah 17:7 KJV).

*The meek also shall increase their joy in the Lord, and the poor among men shall rejoice in the Holy One of Israel* (Isaiah 29:19 KJV).

*But when he seeth his children, the work of Mine hands, in the midst of him, they shall sanctify My name, and sanctify the Holy One of Jacob, and shall fear the God of Israel* (Isaiah 29:23 KJV).

*Get you out of the way, turn aside out of the path, cause the Holy One of Israel to cease from before us* (Isaiah 30:11 KJV).

*Wherefore thus saith the Holy One of Israel, Because ye despise this word, and trust in oppression and perverseness, and stay thereon* (Isaiah 30:12 KJV).

*For thus saith the Lord God, the Holy One of Israel; In returning and rest shall ye be saved; in quietness and in confidence shall be your strength: and ye would not* (Isaiah 30:15 KJV).

*Woe to them that go down to Egypt for help; and stay on horses, and trust in chariots, because they are many; and in horsemen, because they are very strong; but they look not unto the Holy One of Israel, neither seek the Lord!* (Isaiah 31:1 KJV)

*Whom hast thou reproached and blasphemed? and against whom hast thou exalted thy voice, and lifted up thine eyes on high? even against the Holy One of Israel* (Isaiah 37:23 KJV).

*To whom then will ye liken Me, or shall I be equal? saith the Holy One* (Isaiah 40:25 KJV).

*Fear not, thou worm Jacob, and ye men of Israel; I will help thee, saith the Lord, and thy Redeemer, the Holy One of Israel* (Isaiah 41:14 KJV).

*Thou shalt fan them, and the wind shall carry them away, and the whirlwind shall scatter them: and thou shalt rejoice in the Lord, and shalt glory in the Holy One of Israel* (Isaiah 41:16 KJV).

*That they may see, and know, and consider, and understand together, that the hand of the Lord hath done this, and the Holy One of Israel hath created it* (Isaiah 41:20 KJV).

*For I am the Lord thy God, the Holy One of Israel, thy Saviour: I gave Egypt for thy ransom, Ethiopia and Seba for thee* (Isaiah 43:3 KJV).

*Thus saith the Lord, your Redeemer, the Holy One of Israel; For your sake I have sent to Babylon, and have brought down all their nobles, and the Chaldeans, whose cry is in the ships* (Isaiah 43:14 KJV).

*I am the Lord, your Holy One, the Creator of Israel, your King* (Isaiah 43:15 KJV).

*Thus saith the Lord, the Holy One of Israel, and his Maker, Ask Me of things to come concerning My sons, and concerning the work of My hands command ye Me* (Isaiah 45:11 KJV).

*As for our Redeemer, the Lord of hosts is His name, the Holy One of Israel* (Isaiah 47:4 KJV).

*Thus saith the Lord, thy Redeemer, the Holy One of Israel; I am the Lord thy God which teacheth thee to profit, which leadeth thee by the way that thou shouldest go* (Isaiah 48:17 KJV).

*Thus saith the Lord, the Redeemer of Israel, and His Holy One, to Him whom man despiseth, to Him whom the nation abhorreth, to a Servant of rulers, Kings shall see and arise, princes also shall worship, because of the Lord that is faithful, and the Holy One of Israel, and He shall choose Thee* (Isaiah 49:7 KJV).

*For thy Maker is thine husband; the Lord of hosts is His name; and thy Redeemer the Holy One of Israel; The God of the whole earth shall He be called* (Isaiah 54:5 KJV).

*Behold, thou shalt call a nation that thou knowest not, and nations that knew not thee shall run unto thee because of the Lord thy God, and for the Holy One of Israel; for He hath glorified thee* (Isaiah 55:5 KJV).

*Surely the isles shall wait for Me, and the ships of Tarshish first, to bring thy sons from far, their silver and their gold with them, unto the name of the Lord thy God, and to the Holy One of Israel, because He hath glorified thee* (Isaiah 60:9 KJV).

*The sons also of them that afflicted thee shall come bending unto thee; and all they that despised thee shall bow themselves down at the soles of thy feet; and they shall call thee, The city of the Lord, The Zion of the Holy One of Israel* (Isaiah 60:14 KJV).

*Call together the archers against Babylon: all ye that bend the bow, camp against it round about; let none thereof escape: recompense her according to her work; according to all that she hath done, do unto her: for she hath been proud against the Lord, against the Holy One of Israel* (Jeremiah 50:29 KJV).

*For Israel hath not been forsaken, nor Judah of his God, of the Lord of hosts; though their land was filled with sin against the Holy One of Israel* (Jeremiah 51:5 KJV).

*So will I make My holy name known in the midst of My people Israel; and I will not let them pollute My holy name any more: and the heathen shall know that I am the Lord, the Holy One in Israel* (Ezekiel 39:7 KJV).

*I saw in the visions of my head upon my bed, and, behold, a watcher and an holy one came down from heaven* (Daniel 4:13 KJV).

*And whereas the king saw a watcher and an holy one coming down from heaven, and saying, Hew the tree down, and destroy it; yet leave the stump of the roots thereof in the earth, even with a band of iron and brass, in the tender grass of the field; and let it be wet with the dew of heaven, and let his portion be with the beasts of the field, till seven times pass over him* (Daniel 4:23 KJV).

*I will not execute the fierceness of Mine anger, I will not return to destroy Ephraim: for I am God, and not man; the Holy One in the midst of thee: and I will not enter into the city* (Hosea 11:9 KJV).

*Art Thou not from everlasting, O Lord my God, mine Holy One? We shall not die. O Lord, Thou hast ordained them for judgment; and, O mighty God, Thou hast established them for correction* (Habakkuk 1:12 KJV).

*God came from Teman, and the Holy One from mount Paran. Selah. His glory covered the heavens, and the earth was full of His praise* (Habakkuk 3:3 KJV).

*Saying, Let us alone; what have we to do with Thee, Thou Jesus of Nazareth? Art Thou come to destroy us? I know Thee who Thou art, the Holy One of God* (Mark 1:24 KJV).

*Saying, Let us alone; what have we to do with Thee, Thou Jesus of Nazareth? Art Thou come to destroy us? I know Thee who Thou art; the Holy One of God* (Luke 4:34 KJV).

*But ye have an unction from the Holy One, and ye know all things* (1 John 2:20 KJV).

# REFERENCES

Graham, Billy. *Angels.* Nashville, Thomas Nelson, 1995.

*Hastings Dictionary of the Bible.* Hendrickson Pub., 1989.

Hayford, Jack W., exec. ed., *Spirit-Filled Life Bible, NKJV.* Nashville: Thomas Nelson, 1991.

Hickey, Marilyn. *Angels All Around.* Englewood, CO: Marilyn Hickey Ministries, 1992.

Phillips, P. *Angels, Angels, Angels.* Starburst, 1993.

Roberts, Oral. *All You Have Ever Wanted to Know About Angels.* Tulsa, OK: Oral Roberts Evangelistic Association, 1994.

Strong, James. *Strong's Exhaustive Concordance of the Bible.* Universal Subject Guide—Angels, p. 14.

Sumrall, Lester. *Angels: The Messengers of God.* South Bend, IN: LeSea Pub., 1993.

*World Book Encyclopedia.* Field Enterprises Educ. Corp., 1973.

# ABOUT THE AUTHORS

Harry and Cheryl Salem travel the world ministering the Gospel, telling people that Jesus loves them and that He is returning soon! Their lives revolve around seeking the Lord and where He would have them go. Two by two they travel, loving God's people, living and moving in His anointing.

In 1999, Harry and Cheryl endured the loss of their 6-year-old daughter, Gabrielle. As they boldly took steps of faith to overcome the agonizing pain of Gabrielle's death, they asked God to restore them and for souls to come into His Kingdom. God has restored the Salem family, and because of His mighty anointing, the altars have been full! Harry and Cheryl are committed to leading godly lives as an example to others. Their two sons, Harry III and Roman, are continuing their education in addition to participating in the family ministry.

Together, Harry and Cheryl have written books and produced numerous music and ministry CDs to help enable believers to not only overcome but to excel in their Christian lives.

They love people and they love pouring themselves out because God's immense mercy, grace, and love keep them filled up in return. They are blessed and privileged to go out, two by two, reaching families one by one (see Luke 10:1-2).

To contact Cheryl and Harry Salem, write:

Salem Family Ministries
PO Box 701287
Tulsa, Oklahoma 74170

*Please include your prayer requests
and comments when you write.*

Website: www.salemfamilyministries.org

## OTHER BOOKS BY HARRY AND CHERYL SALEM

*Don't Kill Each Other! Let God Do It!*

*We Who Worship*

*Entering Rest—Be Still (A 40-Day Journey into the Presence of God)*

*Obtaining Peace—A 40-Day Prayer Journal*

*2 Becoming 1*

*The Choice Is Yours*

*Overcoming Fear—A 40-Day Prayer Journal*

*Every Body Needs Balance*

*From Grief to Glory*

*From Mourning to Morning*

*Distractions from Destiny*

*Speak the Word Over Your Family for Finances*

*Speak the Word Over Your Family for Healing*

*Speak the Word Over Your Family for Salvation*

*Covenant Conquerors*

*Warriors of the Word*

*Fight in the Heavenlies\**

*It's Too Soon to Give Up\**

*Being #1 at Being #2*

*For Men Only*

*A Royal Child*

*The Mommy Book*

*How to Get a Balanced Body**

*Simple Facts; Salvation, Healing & the Holy Ghost**

*Health & Beauty Secrets**

*Choose to be Happy**

*Abuse...Bruised but Not Broken*

*You Are Somebody*

*A Bright Shining Place—The Story of a Miracle*

*Call for availability

# IN THE RIGHT HANDS, THIS BOOK WILL CHANGE LIVES!

Most of the people who need this message will not be looking for this book. To change their lives, you need to put a copy of this book in their hands.

> *But others (seeds) fell into good ground, and brought forth fruit, some a hundred-fold, some sixty-fold, some thirty-fold* (Matthew 13:8).

Our ministry is constantly seeking methods to find the good ground, the people who need this anointed message to change their lives. Will you help us reach these people?

> *Remember this—a farmer who plants only a few seeds will get a small crop. But the one who plants generously will get a generous crop* (2 Corinthians 9:6).

## EXTEND THIS MINISTRY BY SOWING
### 3 BOOKS, 5 BOOKS, 10 BOOKS, **OR MORE TODAY,**
#### AND BECOME A LIFE CHANGER!

Thank you,

*[signature]*

Don Nori Sr., Publisher
Destiny Image
Since 1982

# DESTINY IMAGE PUBLISHERS, INC.

*"Speaking to the Purposes of God for This Generation
and for the Generations to Come."*

## VISIT OUR NEW SITE HOME AT
## WWW.DESTINYIMAGE.COM

---

## FREE SUBSCRIPTION TO DI NEWSLETTER

Receive free unpublished articles by top DI authors, exclusive
discounts, and free downloads from our best and newest books.
**Visit www.destinyimage.com to subscribe.**

---

Write to:     Destiny Image
              P.O. Box 310
              Shippensburg, PA 17257-0310

Call:      1-800-722-6774

Email:      orders@destinyimage.com

For a complete list of our titles or to place an order
online, visit www.destinyimage.com.

FIND US ON FACEBOOK OR FOLLOW US ON TWITTER.

www.facebook.com/destinyimage     facebook
www.twitter.com/destinyimage      twitter

Made in United States
Orlando, FL
18 August 2022

21236486R00166